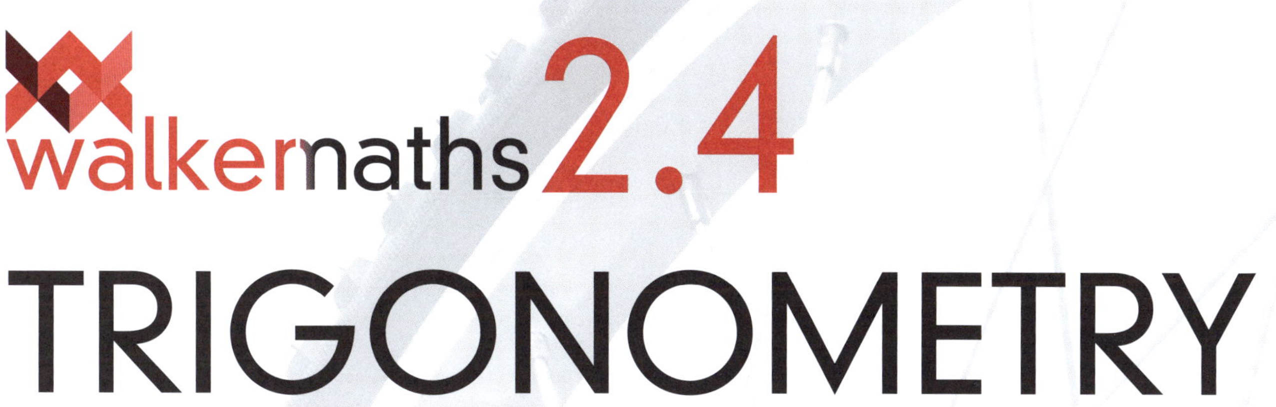

TRIGONOMETRY

NCEA Level 2 Internal

Charlotte Walker and Victoria Walker

Walker Maths 2.4 Trigonometry
1st Edition
Charlotte Walker
Victoria Walker

Editor: Eva Chan
Cover and Text design: Cheryl Smith, Macarn Design
Production controller: Siew Han Ong
Reprint: Jess Lovell

Acknowledgements
Cover photo courtesy of Shutterstock.

For product information and technology assistance,
in Australia call **1300 790 853**;
in New Zealand call **0800 449 725**

For permission to use material from this text or product, please email
aust.permissions@cengage.com

National Library of New Zealand Cataloguing-in-Publication Data
A catalogue record for this book is available from the National Library of New Zealand.

ISBN 978 0 17 035421 9

Cengage Learning Australia
Level 7, 80 Dorcas Street
South Melbourne, Victoria Australia 3205

Cengage Learning New Zealand
Unit 4B Rosedale Office Park
331 Rosedale Road, Albany, North Shore 0632, NZ

For learning solutions, visit **cengage.co.nz**

Printed in China by 1010 Printing International Limited.
20 25

CONTENTS

ISBN: 9780170354219

Formulae

These are the formulae for this achievement standard. Remember to check with your teacher to see which ones you will be provided with in your assessment.

Sine rule (sides)	$\frac{a}{\sin A} = \frac{b}{\sin B} = \frac{c}{\sin C}$
Sine rule (angles)	$\frac{\sin A}{a} = \frac{\sin B}{b} = \frac{\sin C}{c}$
Cosine rule (sides)	$a^2 = b^2 + c^2 - 2bc \cos A$
Cosine rule (angles)	$\cos A = \frac{b^2 + c^2 - a^2}{2bc}$
Area of a triangle	$\frac{1}{2} bc \sin A$
Arc length	$2\pi r \frac{\theta}{360}$
Area of a sector	$\pi r^2 \frac{\theta}{360}$

 ISBN: 9780170354219

Glossary

Make your own glossary of key terms:

Term	Definition	Picture/Example
Pythagoras		
Hypotenuse		
Opposite		
Adjacent		
Equilateral		
Isosceles		
Sector		
Segment		
Arc		

ISBN: 9780170354219

Right-angled triangles

Pythagoras

We use Pythagoras's theorem to find unknown sides on right-angled triangles.

Pythagoras's theorem is: $a^2 + b^2 = c^2$

a and *b* are the short sides; *c* is always the longest side, or hypotenuse.

Example one: Find the longest side (*x*).

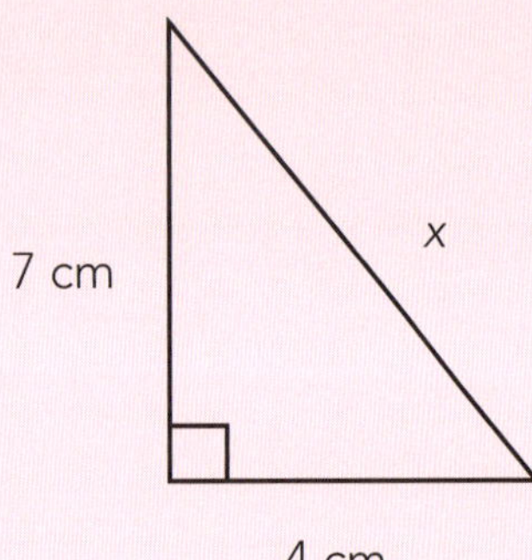

$$a^2 + b^2 = c^2$$
$$4^2 + 7^2 = x^2$$
$$\sqrt{4^2 + 7^2} = x$$
$$x = \sqrt{65}$$
$$x = 8.06 \text{ cm (2 dp)}$$

Example two: Find the missing side (*y*).

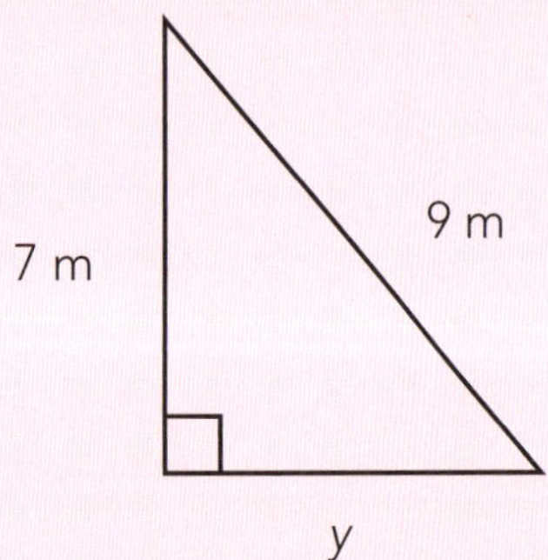

$$a^2 + b^2 = c^2$$
$$y^2 + 7^2 = 9^2$$
$$y^2 = 9^2 - 7^2$$
$$y = \sqrt{9^2 - 7^2}$$
$$y = 5.66 \text{ m (2 dp)}$$

1

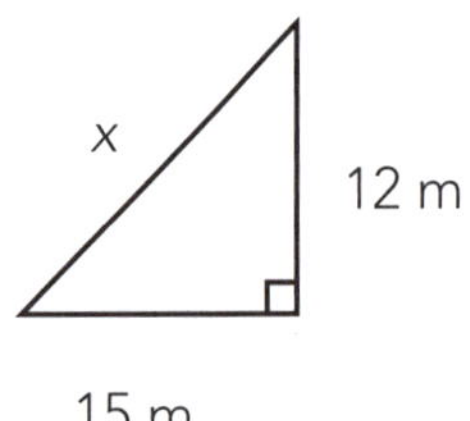

2

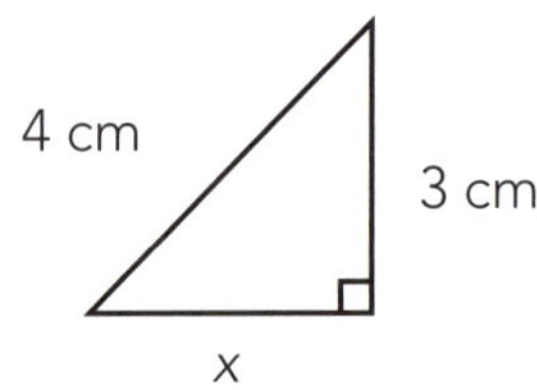

 ISBN: 9780170354219

3

x
11 cm
5 cm

4

12 cm
9 cm
x

5

7 km
x
4 km

6

4.1 m
5.6 m
x

7

3 km
400 m
x

8

16 m
12 m
x

9

456 m
231 m
x

10

x
30 mm
30 mm

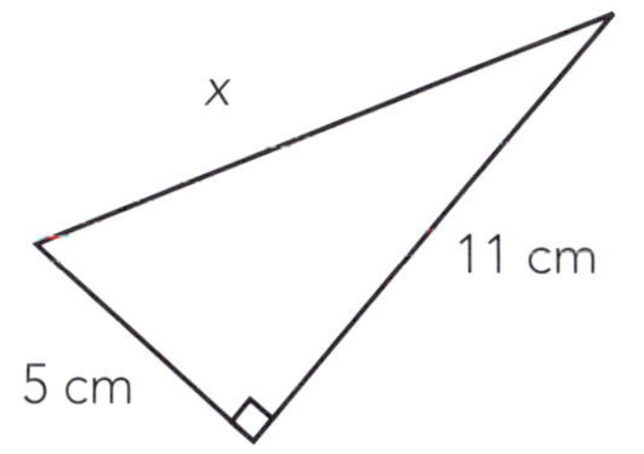

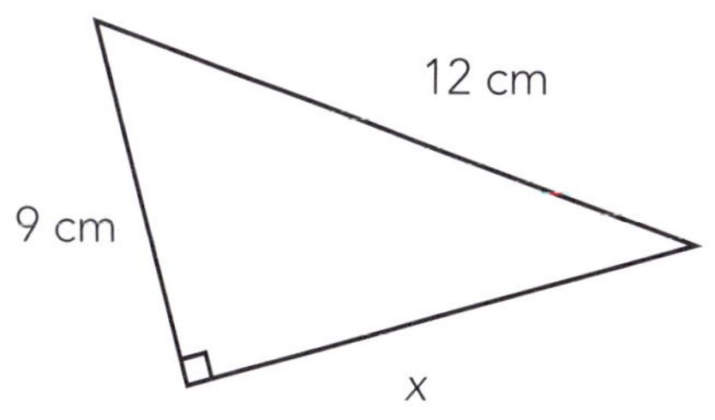

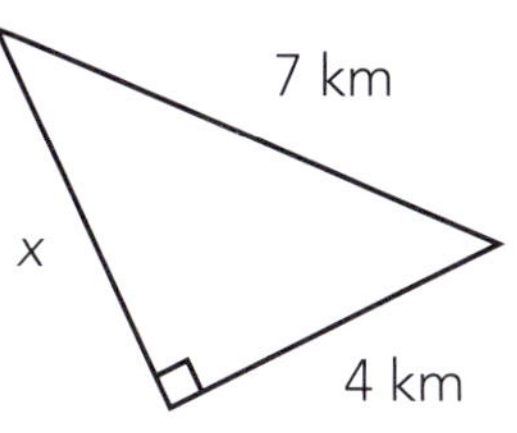

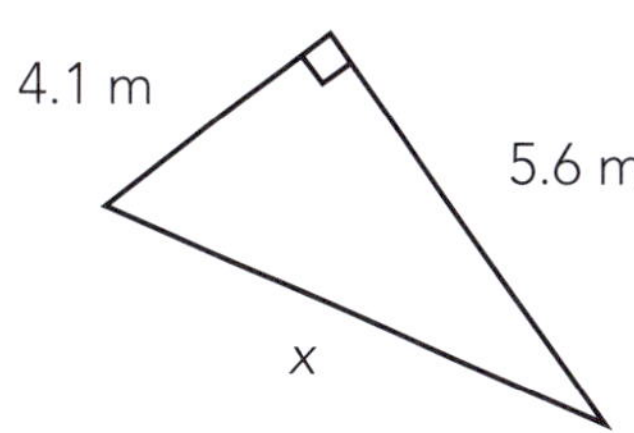

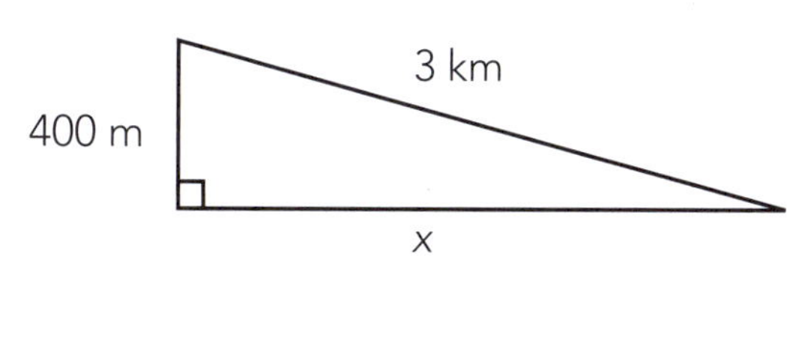

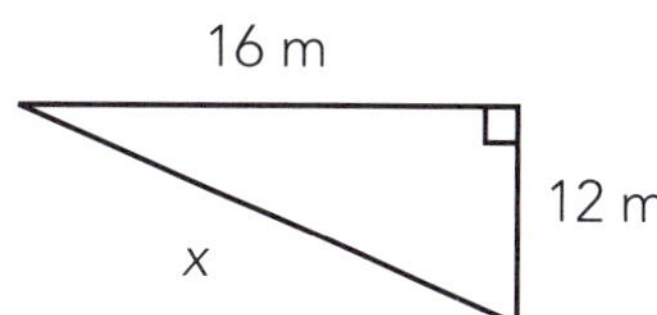

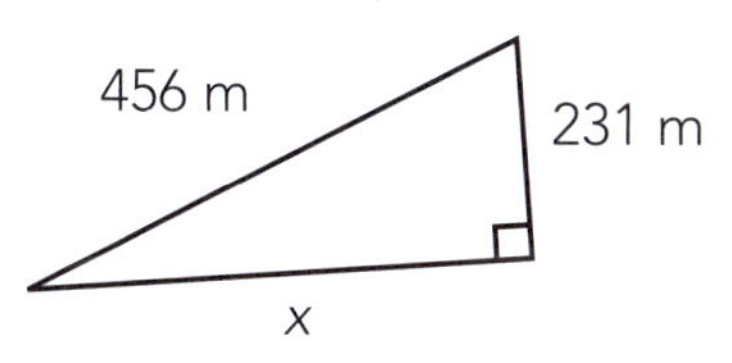

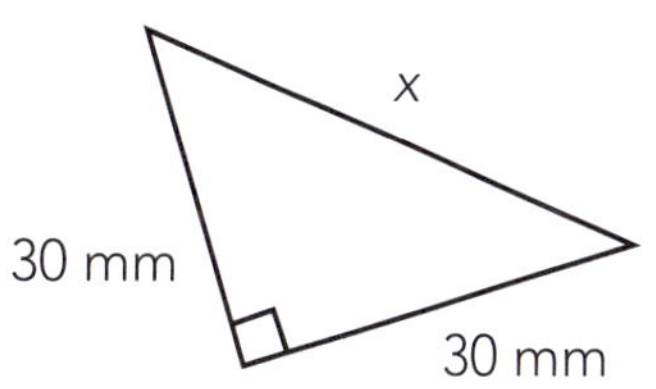

11 ABCD is a square.
Calculate the length of AE.

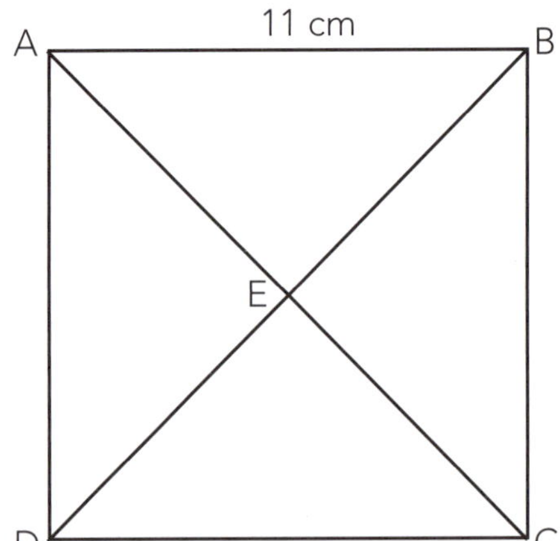

12 ABCD is a trapezium.
Calculate the length of BC.

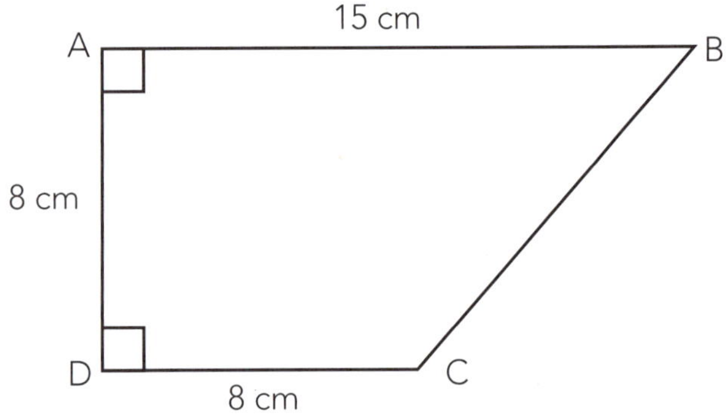

13 Calculate the length of AD.

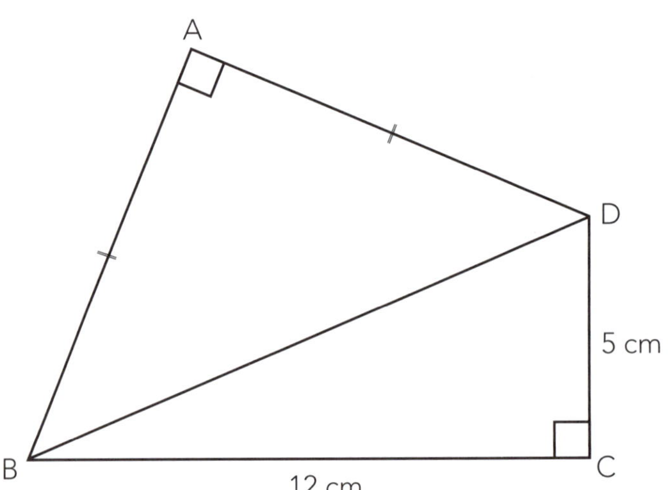

ISBN: 9780170354219

Trigonometry — finding sides

We use trigonometry to find unknown sides and angles of right-angled triangles.

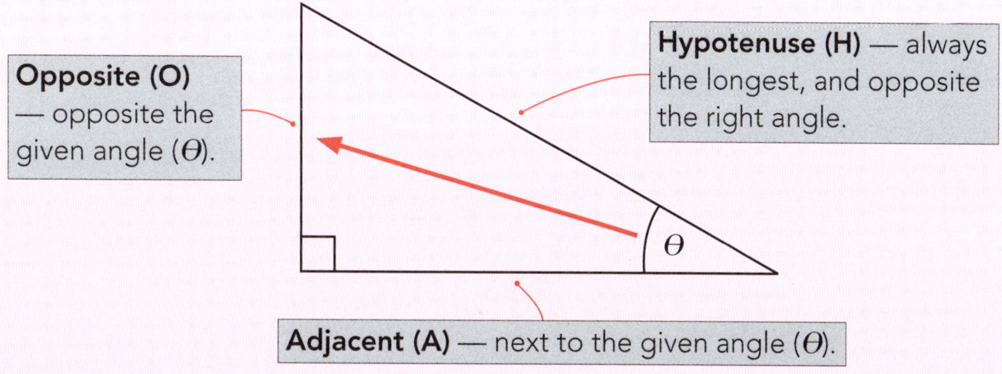

The three rules are:

$$\sin\theta = \frac{O}{H} \qquad \cos\theta = \frac{A}{H} \qquad \tan\theta = \frac{O}{A}$$

Example one: Find the missing side (x).

First, label the sides with O, A and H.

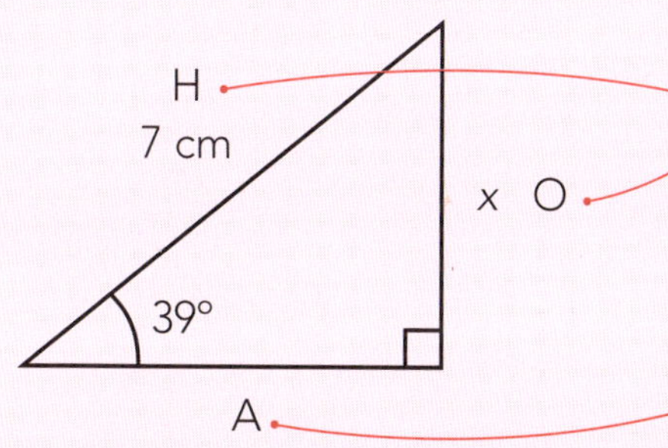

We use these two sides. The opposite side is the one we want to find and the hypotenuse has a measurement.

This side is 'lonely' and therefore of no use to us.

As we are using O and H, we must use the formula:

$$\sin\theta = \frac{O}{H}$$

$$\sin 39° = \frac{x}{7}$$

Substitute the values we know.

$$\sin 39° \times 7 = x$$

$$x = 4.41 \text{ cm (2 dp)}$$

Does this sound sensible?

ISBN: 9780170354219

Example two: Find the longest side (*y*).

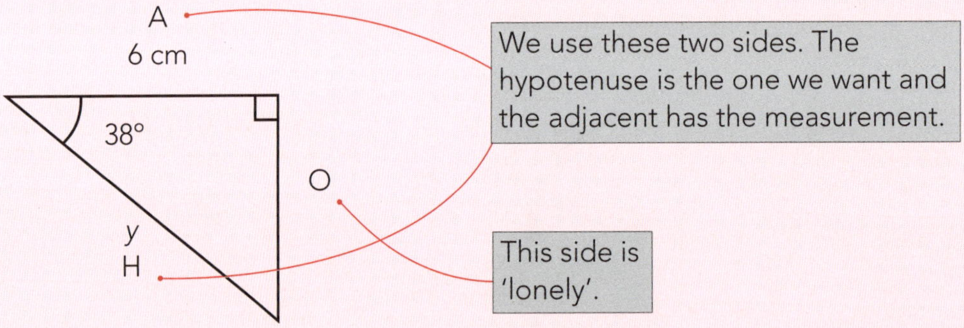

A
6 cm
38°
O
y
H
We use these two sides. The hypotenuse is the one we want and the adjacent has the measurement.
This side is 'lonely'.

As we are using A and H, we must use the formula:

$$\cos \theta = \frac{A}{H}$$

$$\cos 38° = \frac{6}{y}$$ Substitute the values we know.

$$\cos 38° \times y = 6$$

$$y = \frac{6}{\cos 38°}$$

$y = 7.61$ cm (2 dp) Does this sound sensible?

Find the missing sides of these triangles.

1

x
45°
15 m

2

4 cm
45°
x

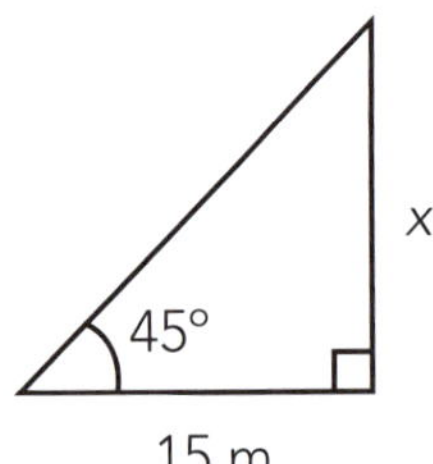

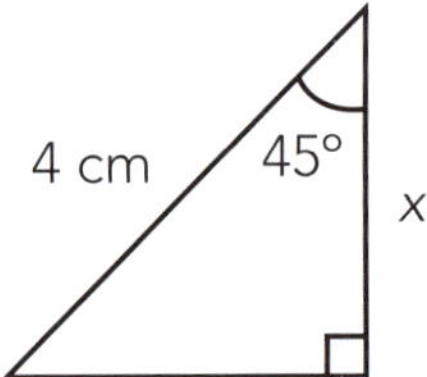

 ISBN: 9780170354219

3

5 cm
28°
x

4

9 cm
34°
x

5

x
48°
4 km

6

x
59°
5.6 m

7

3 km
x
14°

8

67°
12 m
x

9

231 m
23°
x

10

x
50°
30 mm

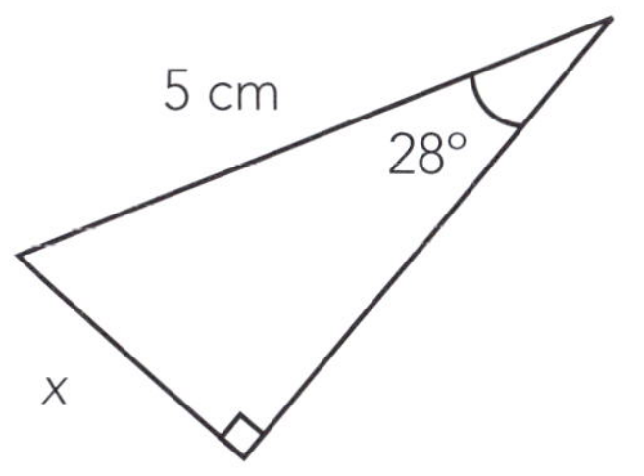

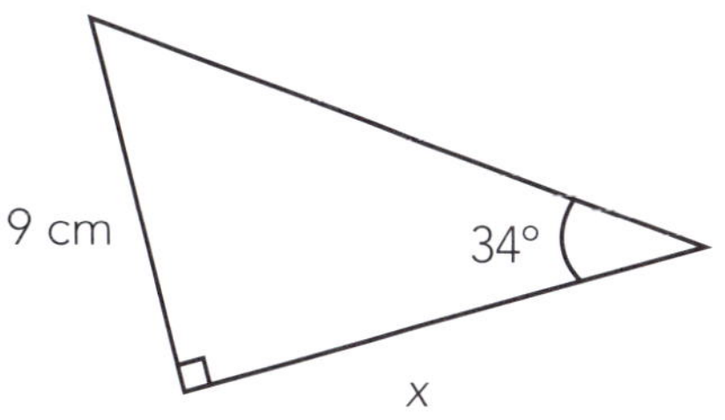

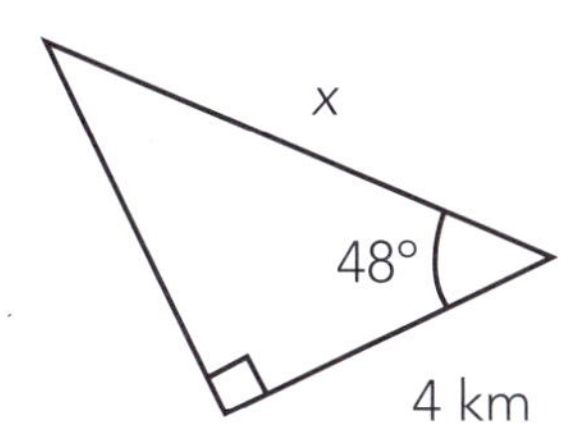

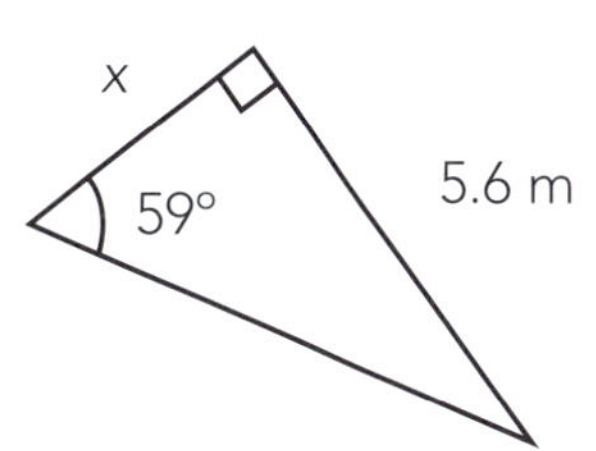

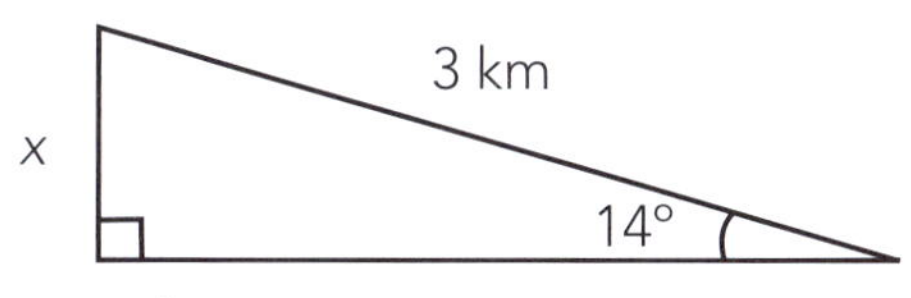

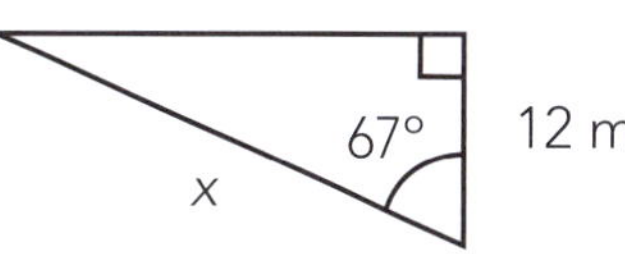

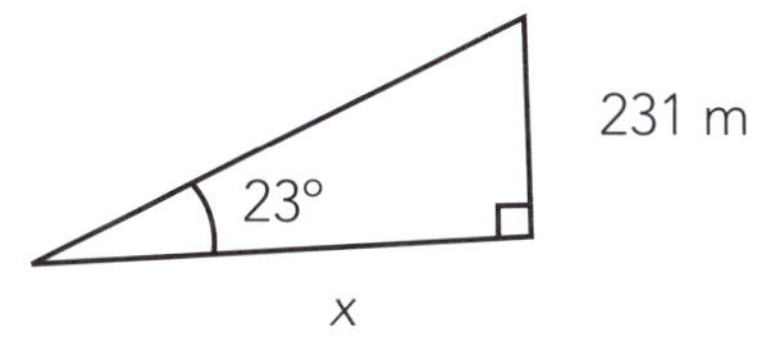

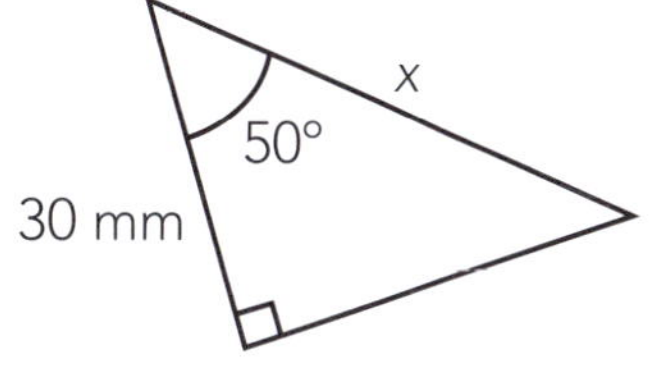

Trigonometry — finding angles

Again we use these three rules:

$$\sin \theta = \frac{O}{H} \qquad \cos \theta = \frac{A}{H} \qquad \tan \theta = \frac{O}{A}$$

Example: Find the marked angle (x).

First, label the sides with O, A and H.

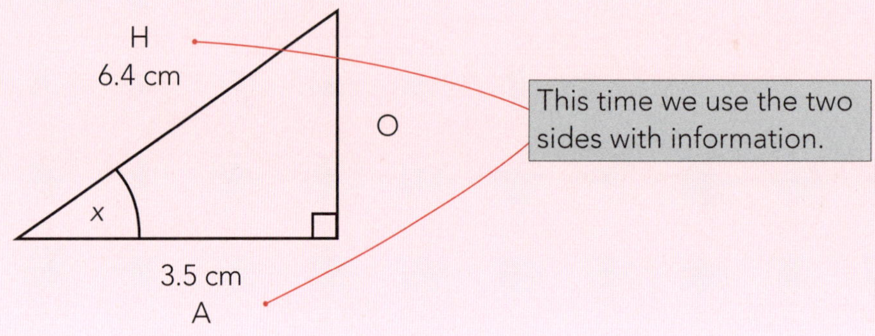

As we are using A and H, we must use the formula:

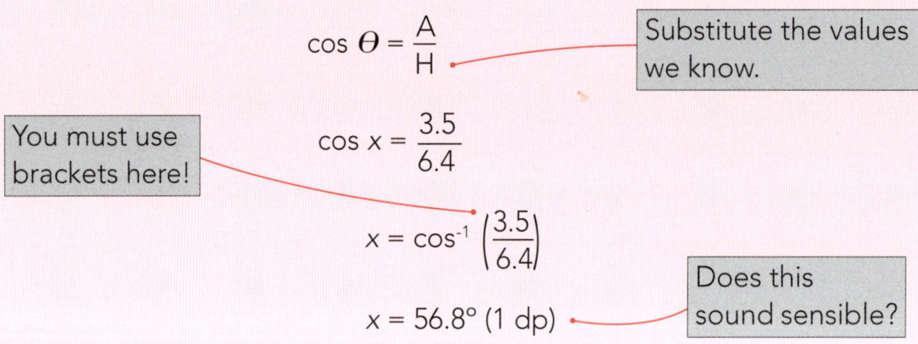

$$\cos \theta = \frac{A}{H}$$

$$\cos x = \frac{3.5}{6.4}$$

$$x = \cos^{-1}\left(\frac{3.5}{6.4}\right)$$

$$x = 56.8° \text{ (1 dp)}$$

Find the missing angles of these triangles.

1

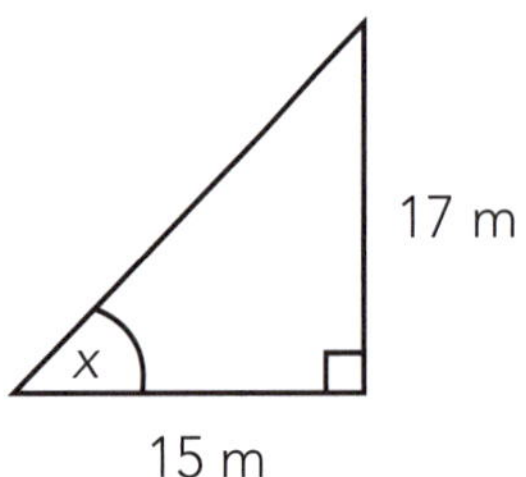

2

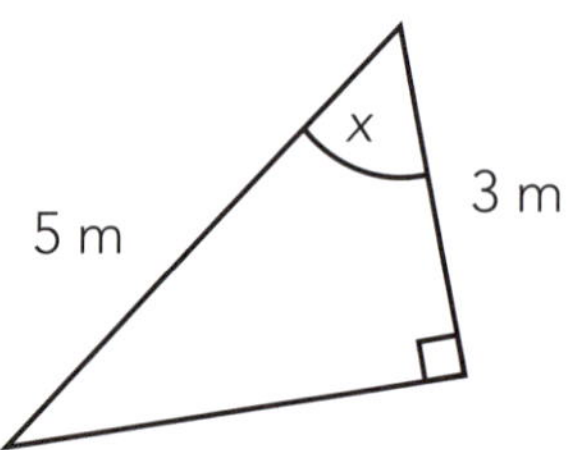

ISBN: 9780170354219

3

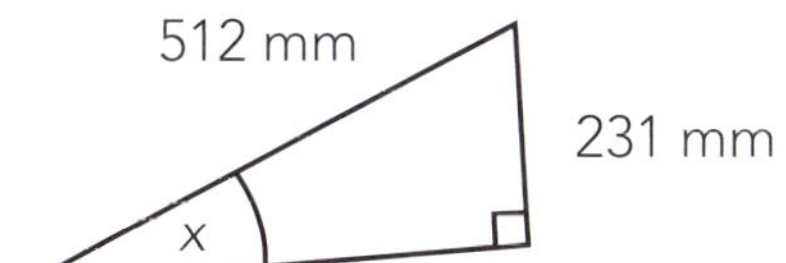

4

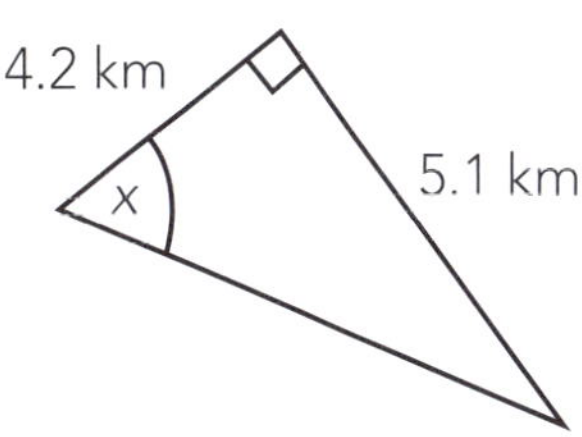

5

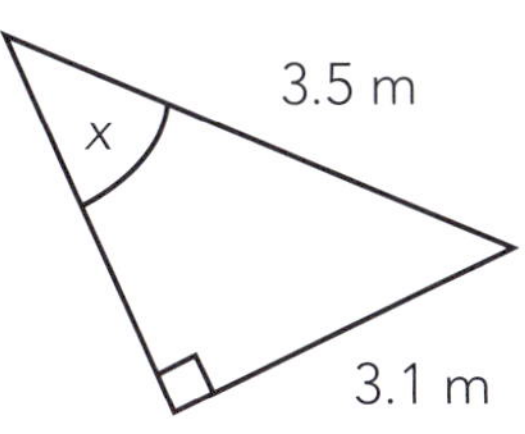

6

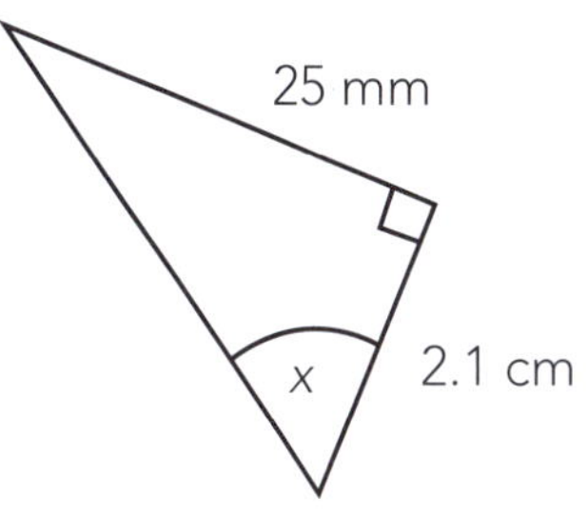

7

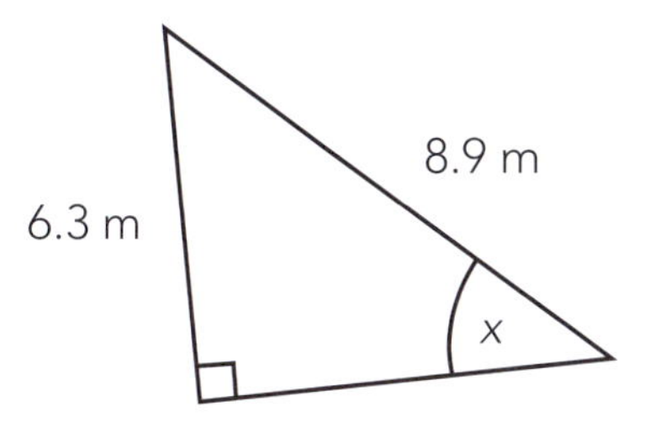

8

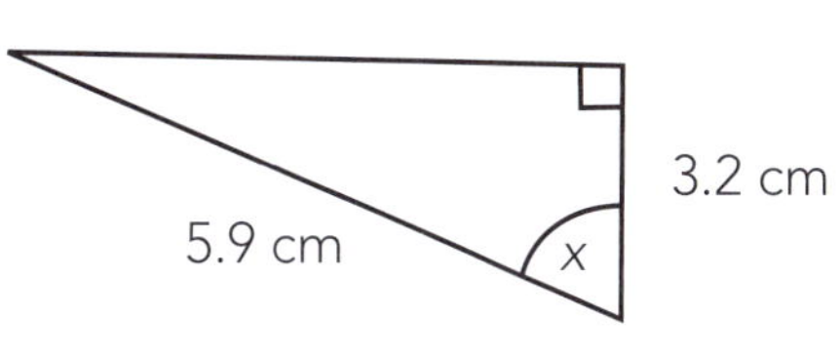

9

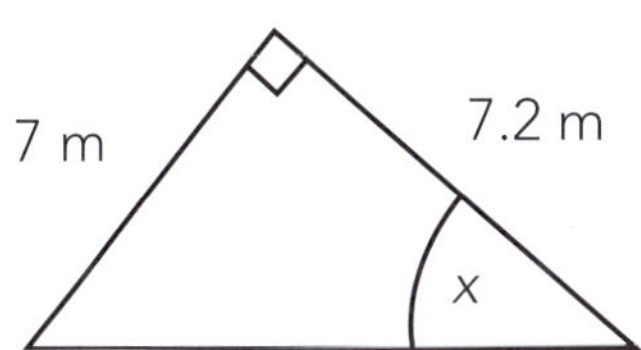

10

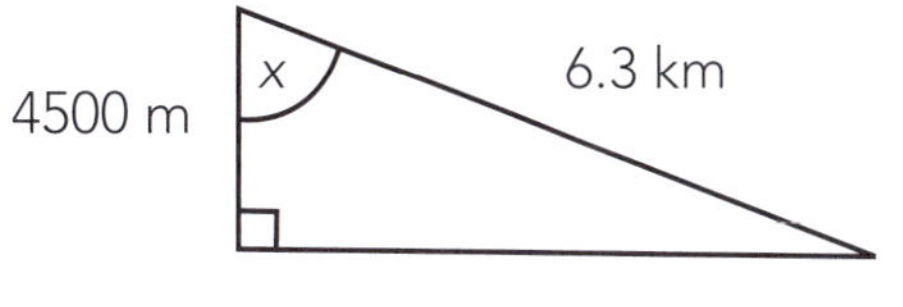

ISBN: 9780170354219

Putting it together

Using the previous two techniques, find the missing sides and angles.

1

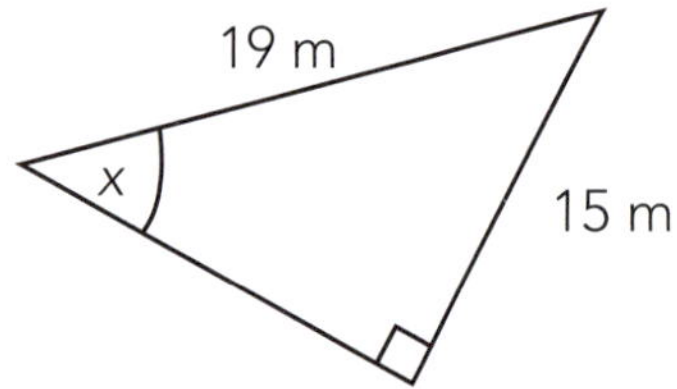

2

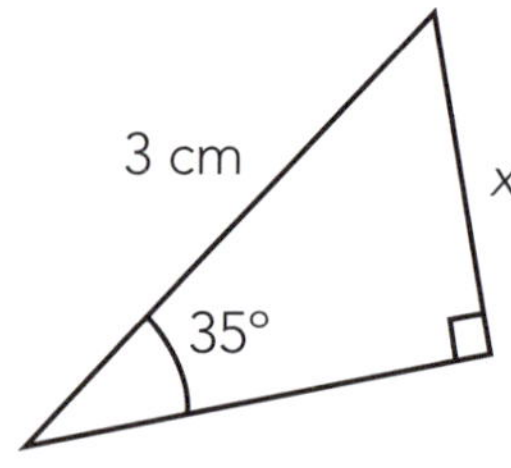

3

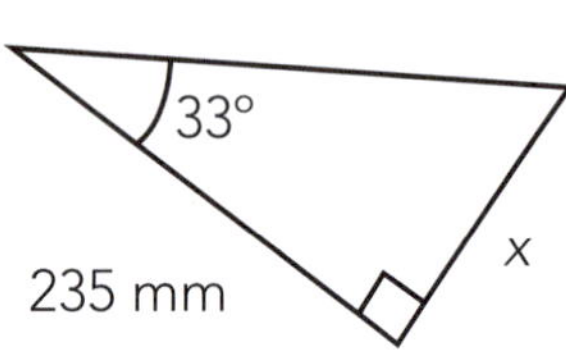

4

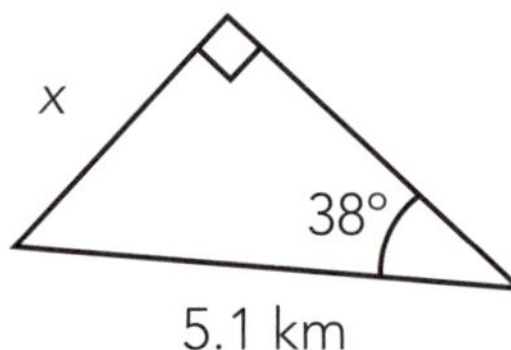

5

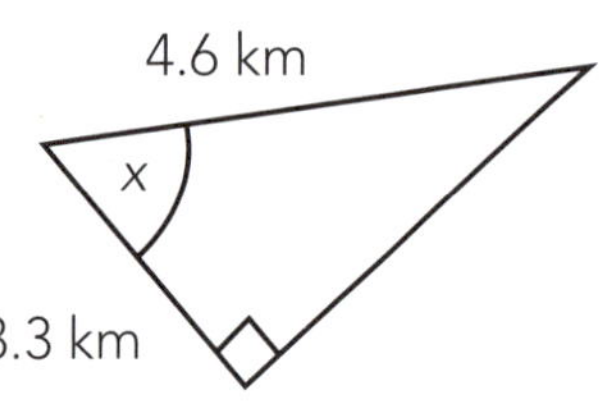

6

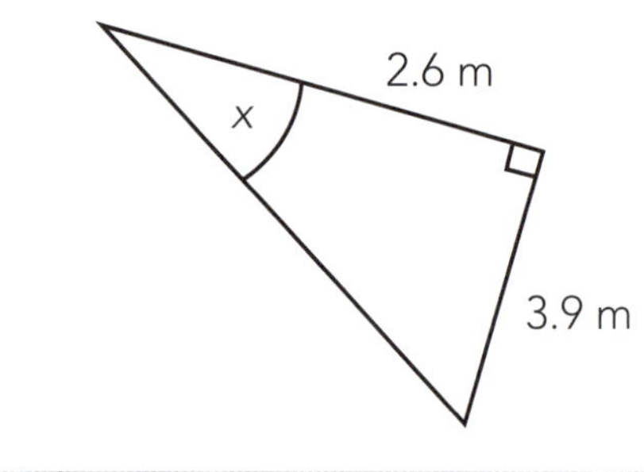

7

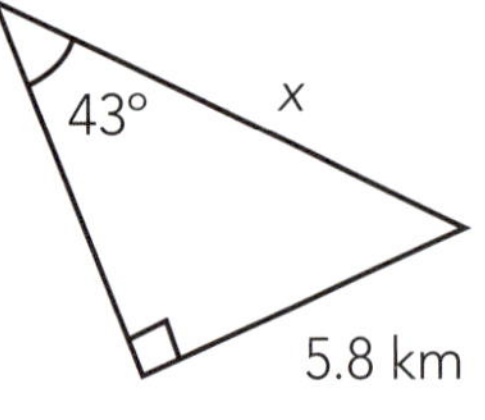

8

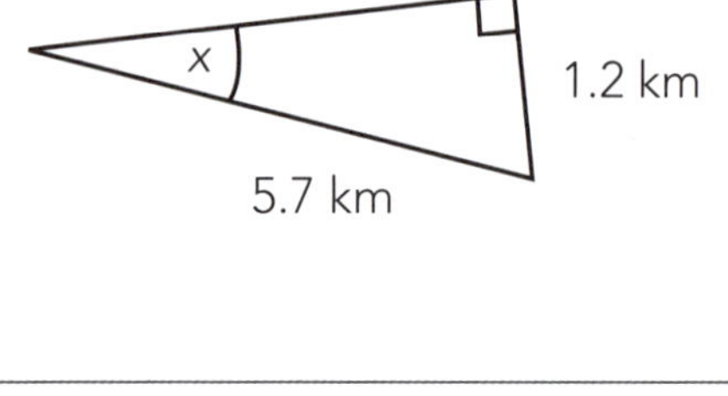

ISBN: 9780170354219

9

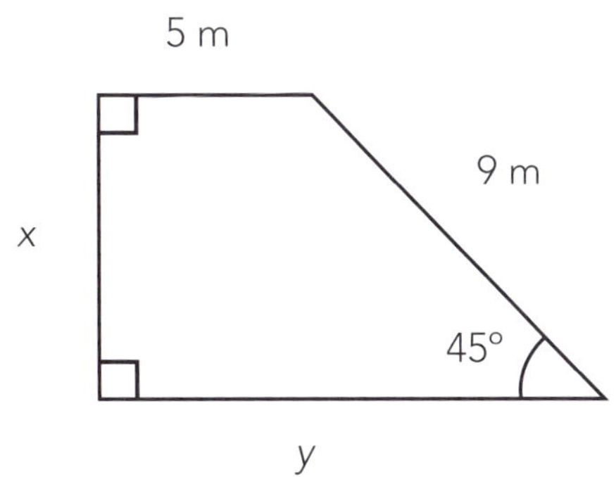

10

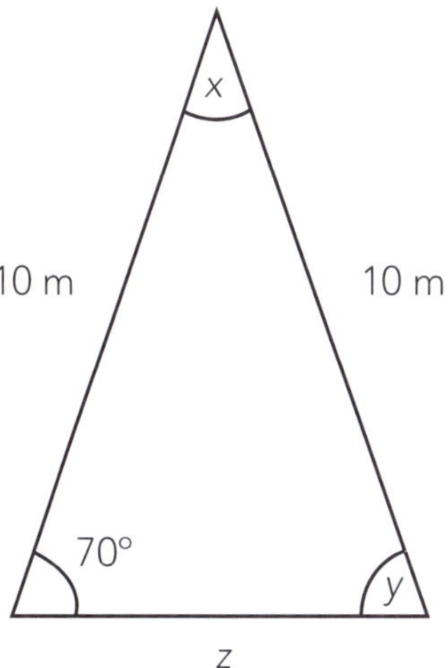

11

What type of quadrilateral is this?

12

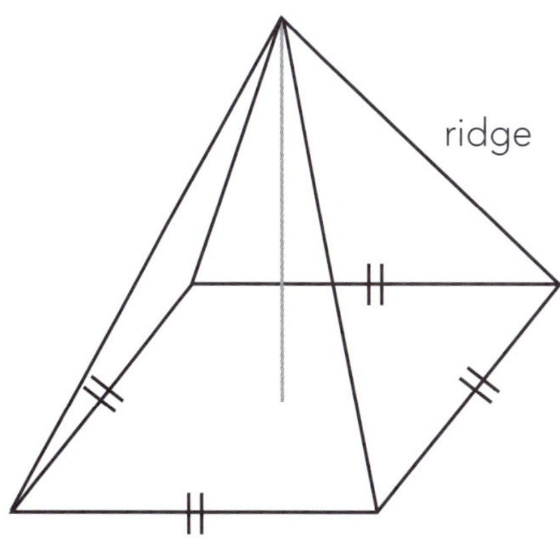

A child's tent has a square floor, with an area of 4 m^2. It is held up by a 2 m pole. How much cord is needed to reinforce the four ridges?

Non-right-angled triangles

Sine rule — finding sides

We use the sine rule when opposites are involved:

$$\frac{a}{\sin A} = \frac{b}{\sin B} = \frac{c}{\sin C}$$

Example: Find the side *x*.

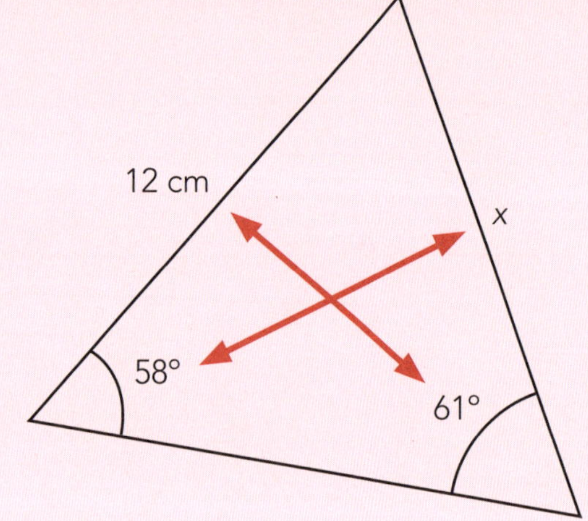

It's important to recognise the opposites here.

We actually use only two of the bits from the equation:

$$\frac{a}{\sin A} = \frac{b}{\sin B}$$

Small letters are sides. Capital letters are angles.

$$\frac{x}{\sin 58°} = \frac{12}{\sin 61°}$$

Substitute what we know. It doesn't matter which one is *a* or *b*.

Rearrange.

$$x = \frac{12}{\sin 61°} \times \sin 58°$$

$$x = 11.64 \text{ cm (2 dp)}$$

ISBN: 9780170354219

Find the missing sides of these triangles.

1

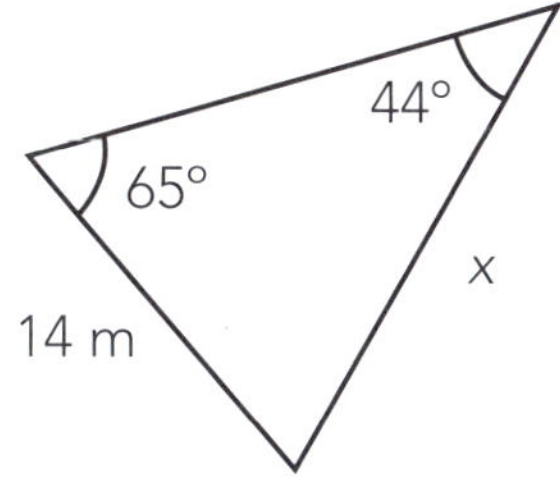

2

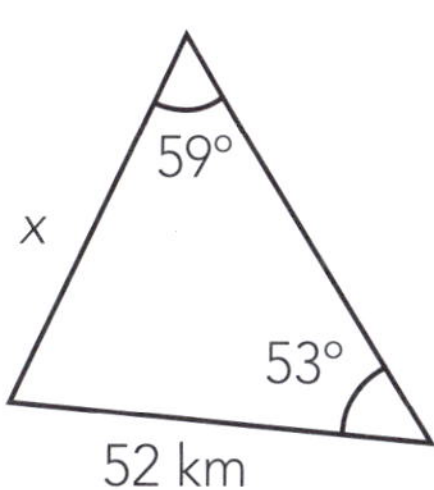

3

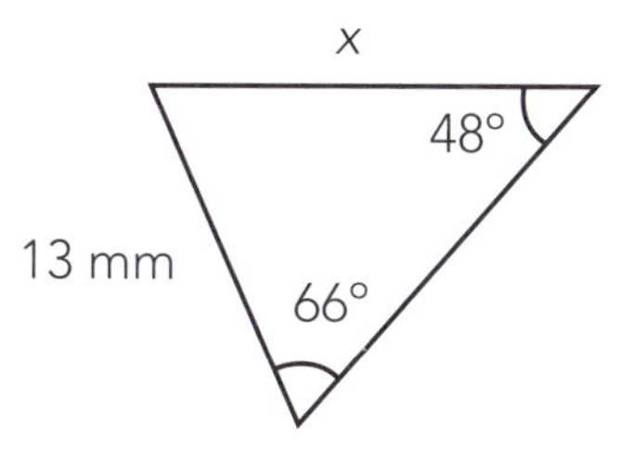

4

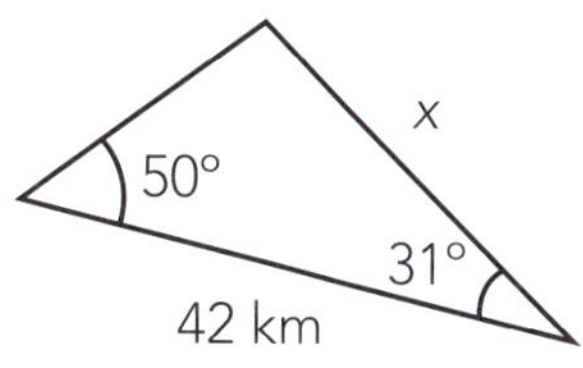

5

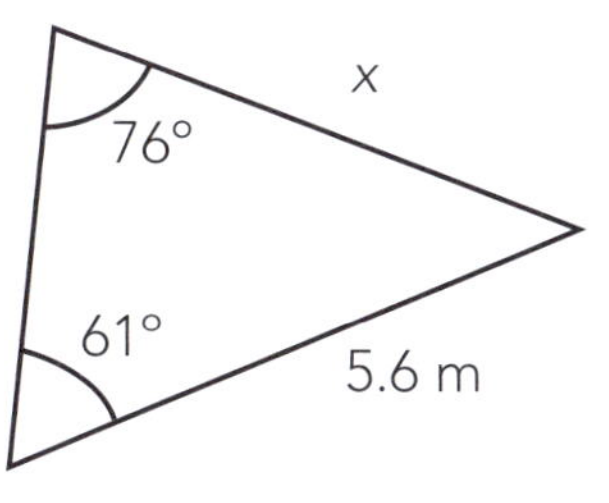

6

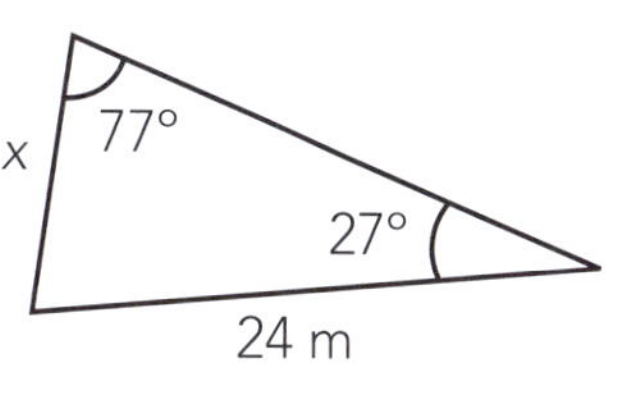

7

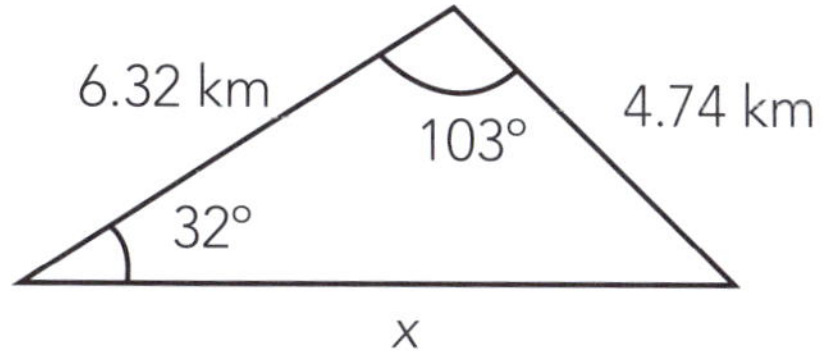

8

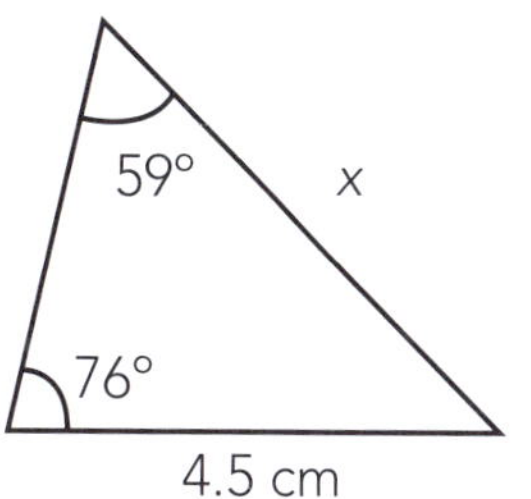

ISBN: 9780170354219

9

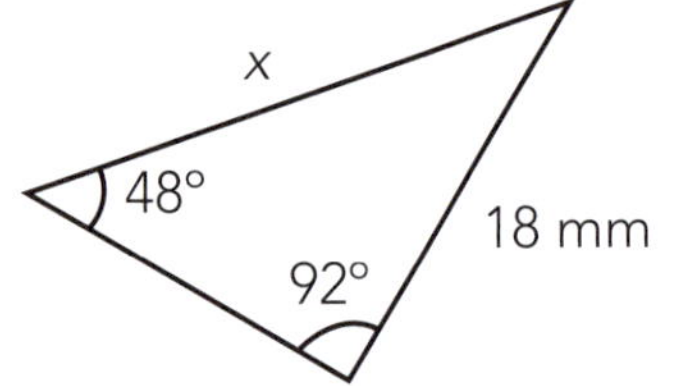

10

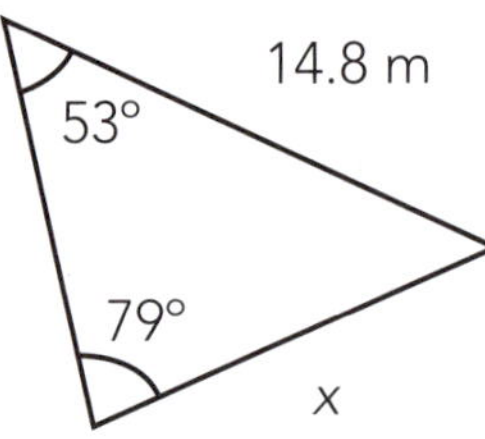

11

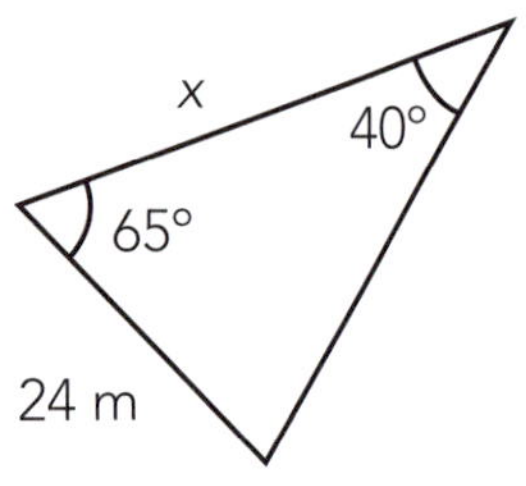

12

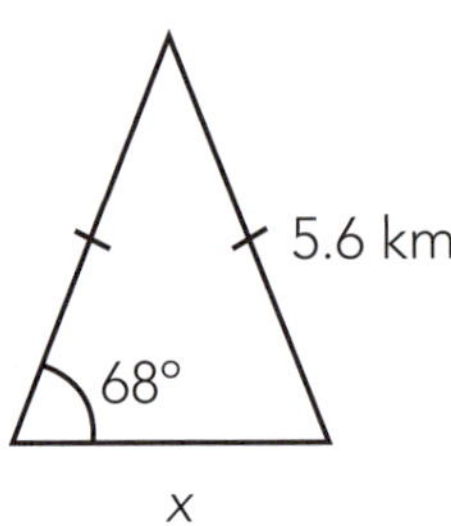

13

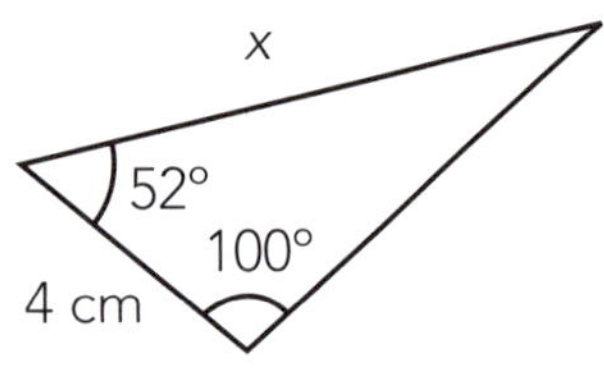

14

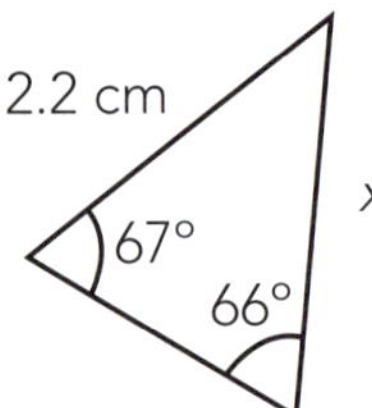

15

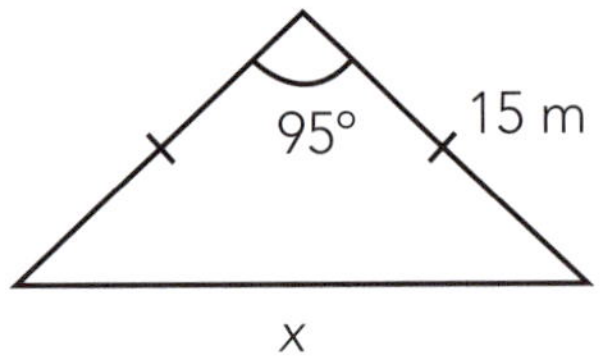

16

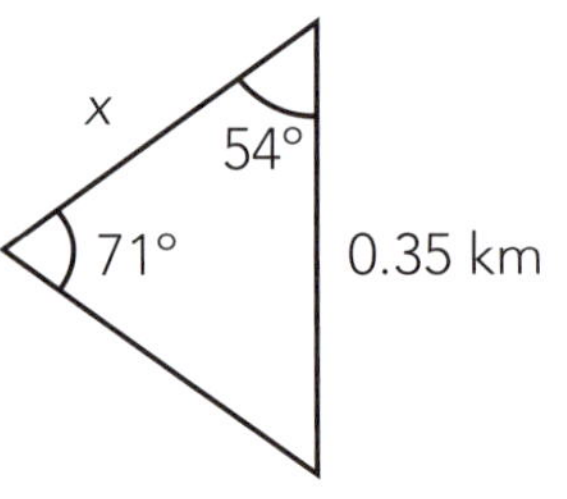

ISBN: 9780170354219

Sine rule — finding angles

We use the same formula to find angles of non-right-angled triangles except we flip it upside down:

$$\frac{\sin A}{a} = \frac{\sin B}{b} = \frac{\sin C}{c}$$

Example: Find the angle x.

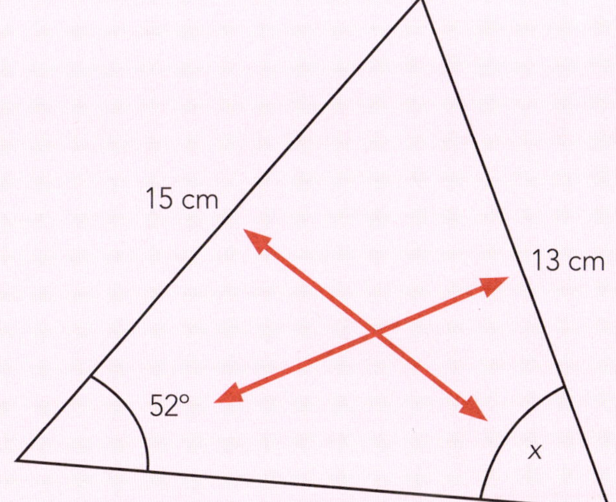

It's important to recognise the opposites here.

We actually use only two of the bits from the equation:

$$\frac{\sin A}{a} = \frac{\sin B}{b}$$

Small letters are sides. Capital letters are angles.

$$\frac{\sin x}{15} = \frac{\sin 52°}{13}$$

Substitute what we know. It doesn't matter which one is *a* or *b*.

Rearrange.

$$\sin x = \frac{\sin 52°}{13} \times 15$$

$$x = \sin^{-1}\left(\frac{\sin 52°}{13} \times 15\right)$$

Good idea to use your 'Ans' button here.

$$x = 65.4° \text{ (1 dp)}$$

ISBN: 9780170354219

Find the missing angles of these triangles.

1

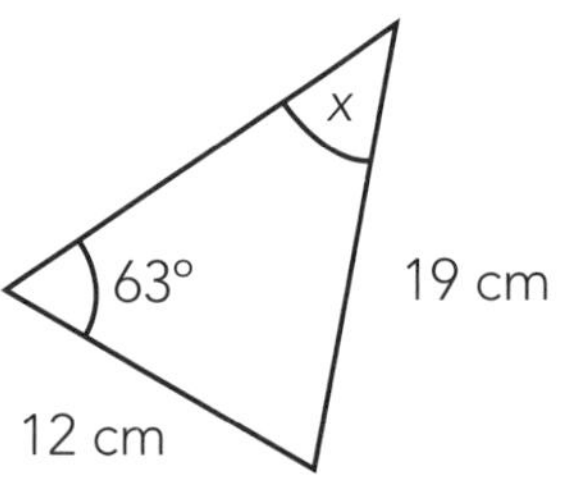

2

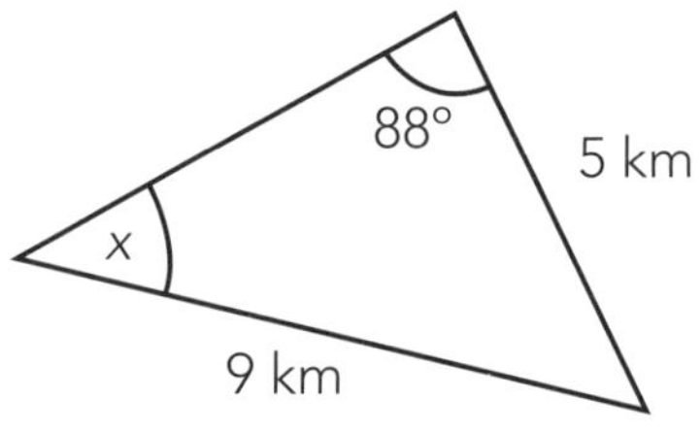

3

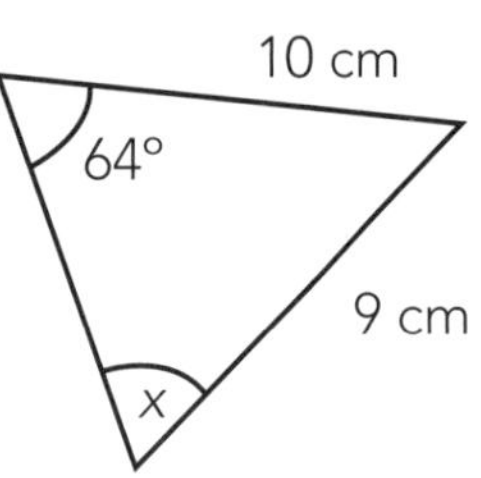

4

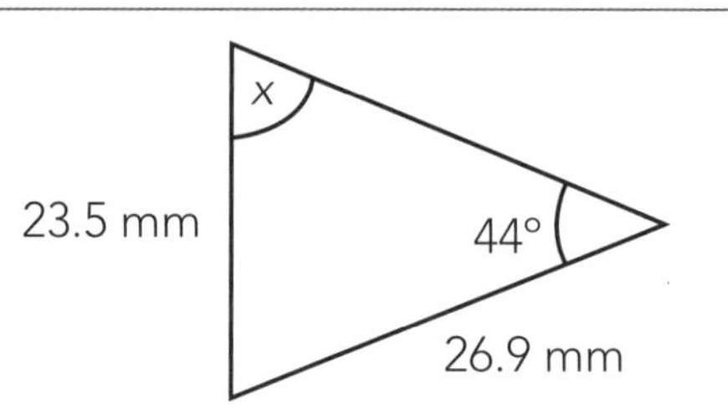

5

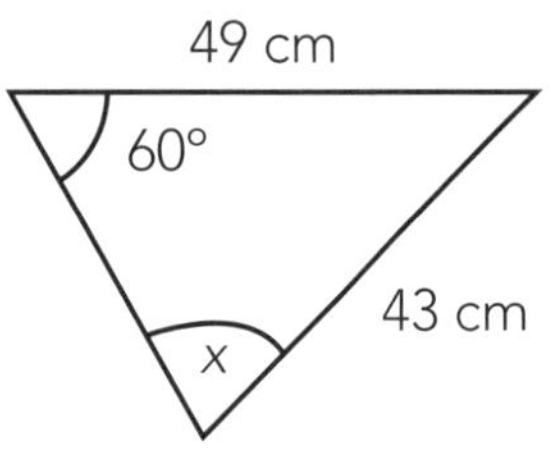

6

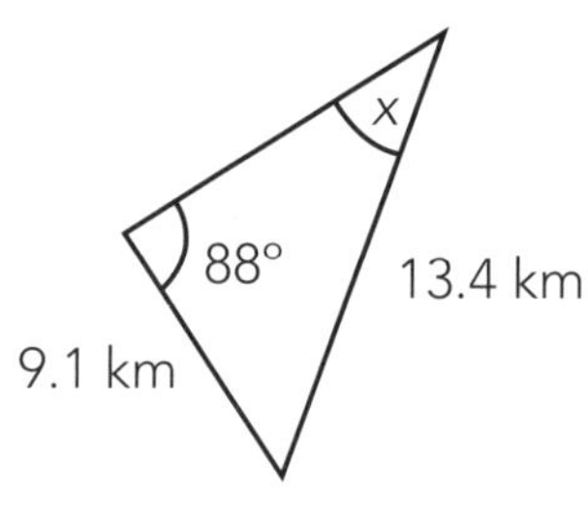

7

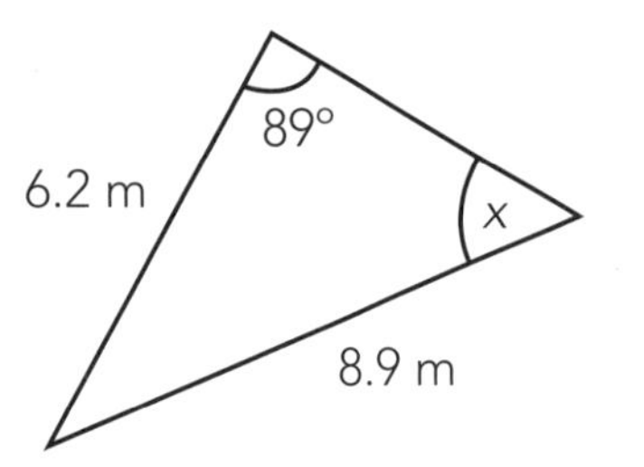

8

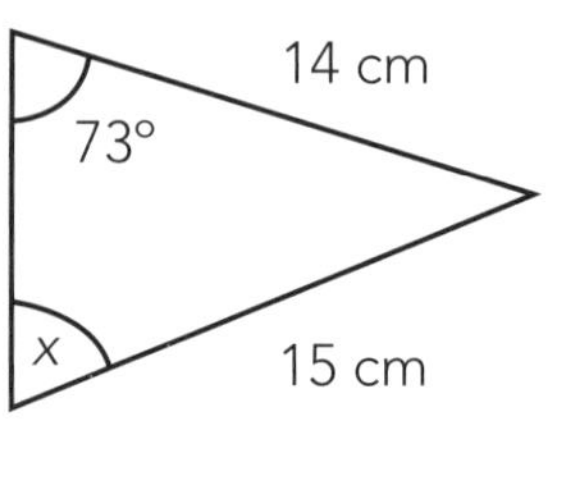

ISBN: 9780170354219

9

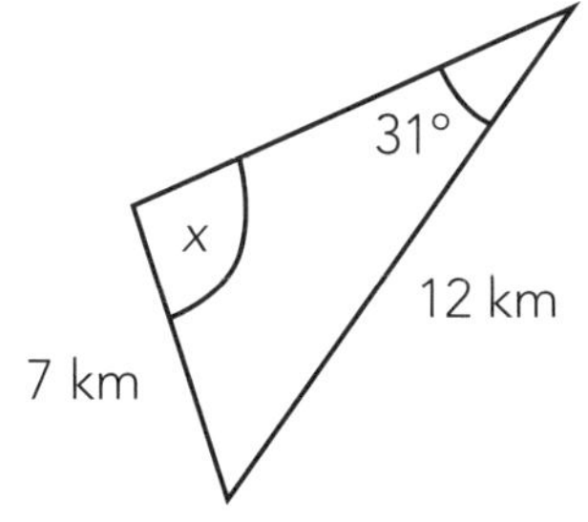

10

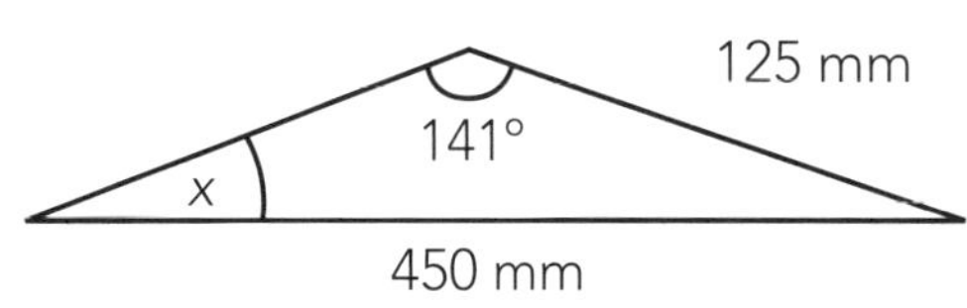

11

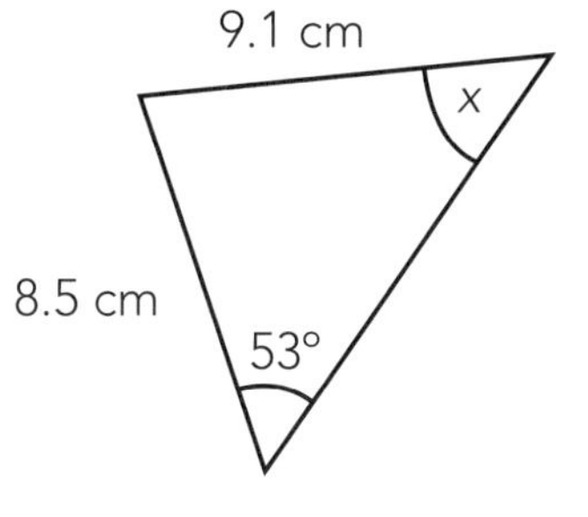

12

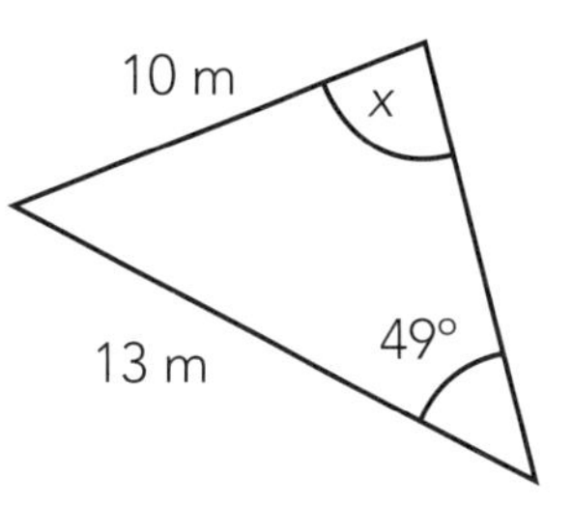

13

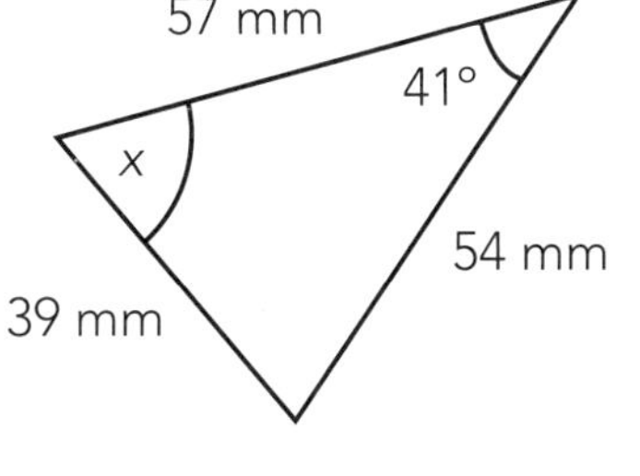

14

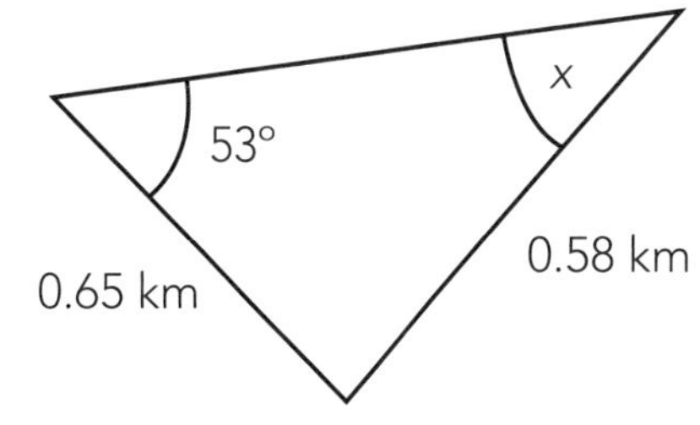

15

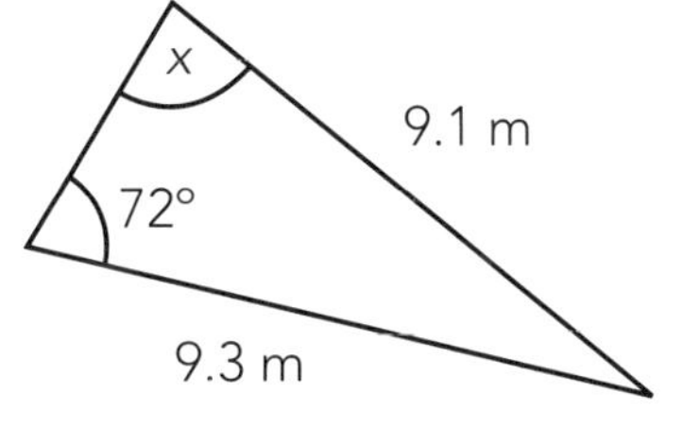

16

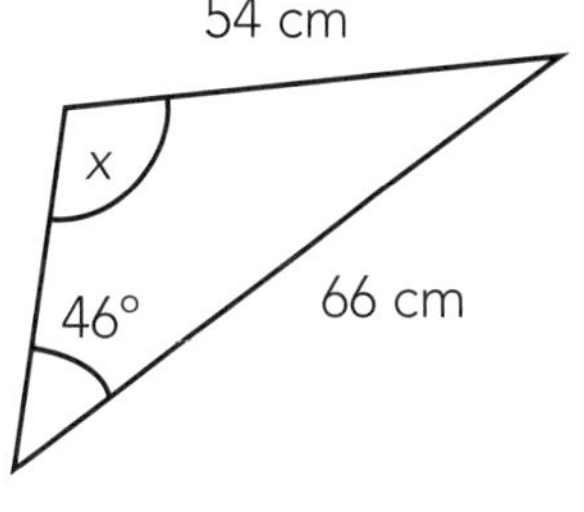

17 Calculate the width of the river (AB).

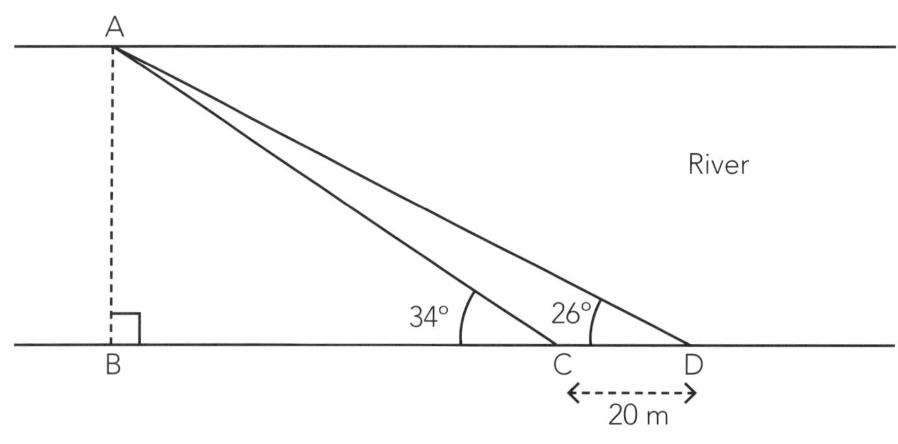

18 Calculate the height of the chimney (AD).

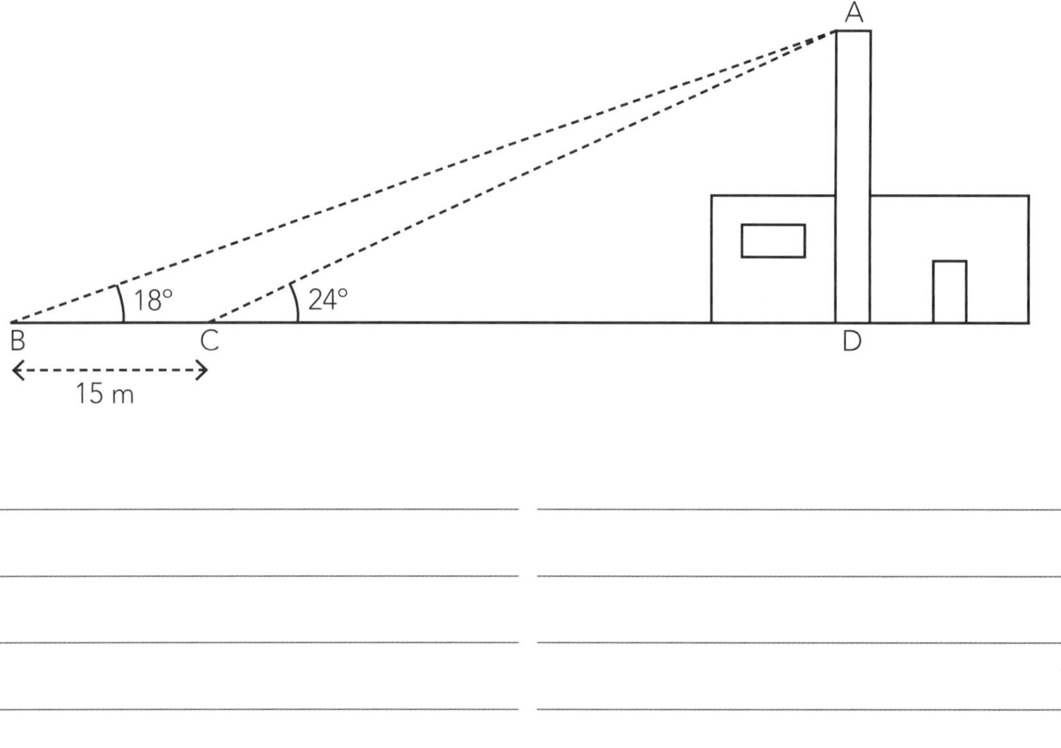

  ISBN: 9780170354219

Cosine rule — finding sides

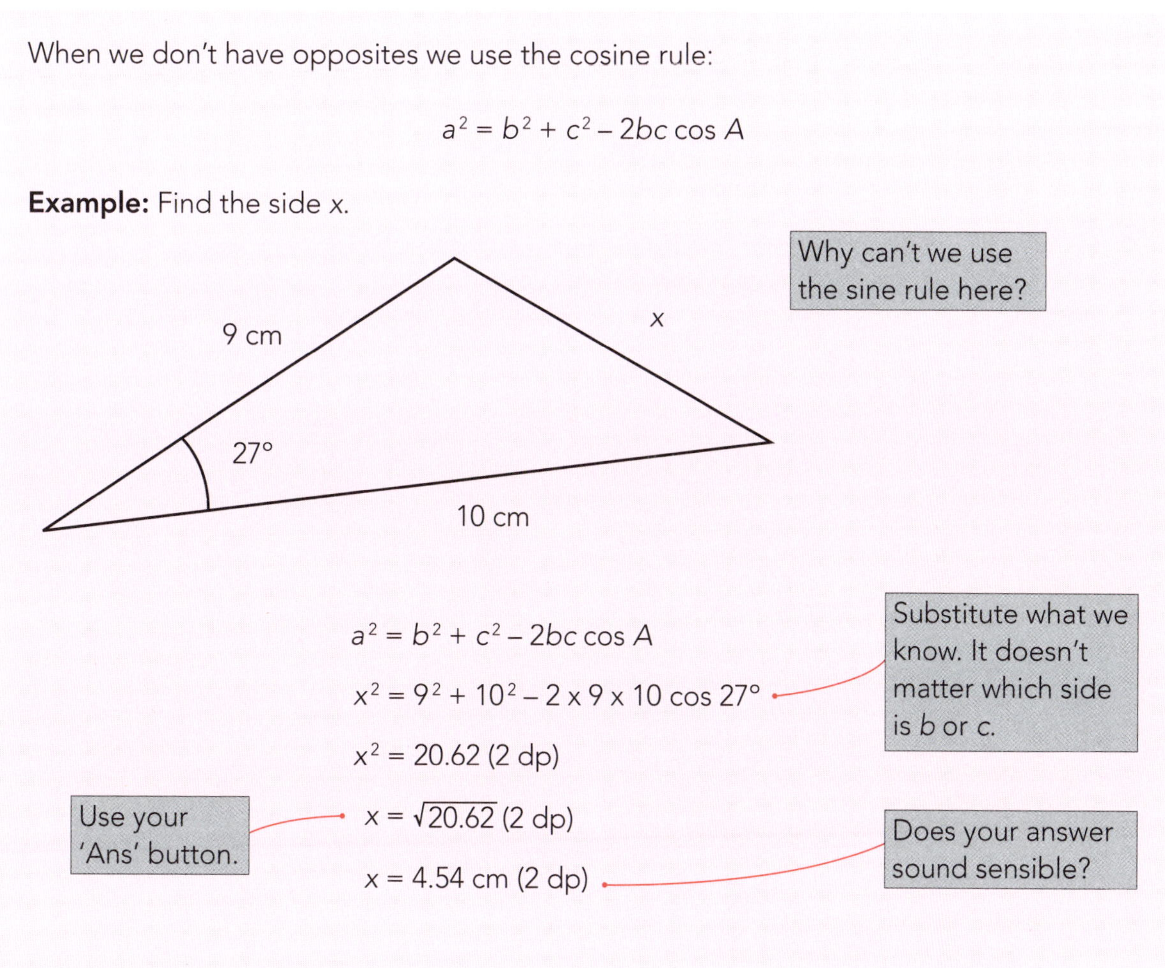

Find the missing sides of these triangles.

1

2.5 cm

74°

1.6 cm

x

2

521 m

69°

500 m

x

ISBN: 9780170354219

3

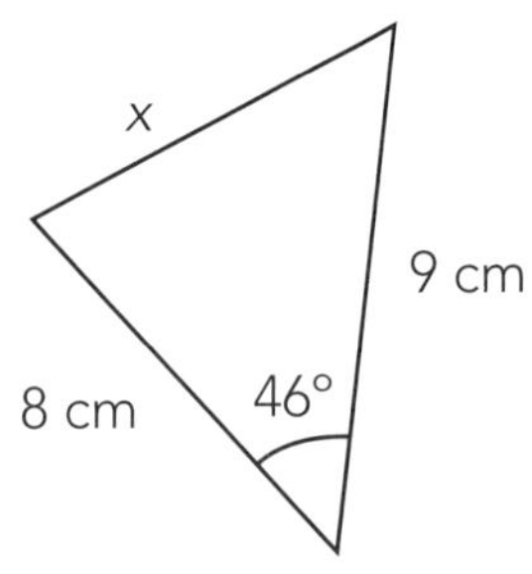

4

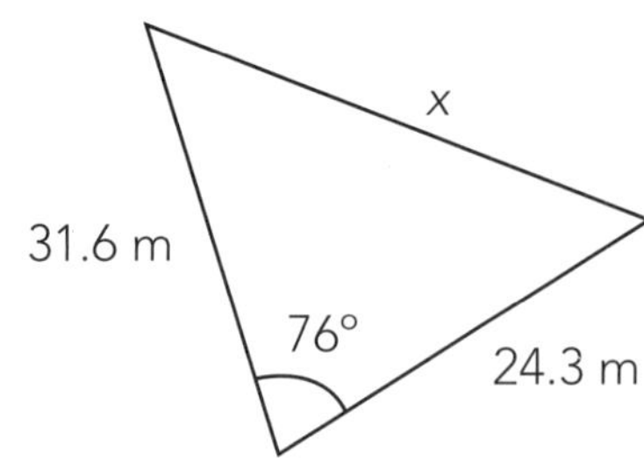

5

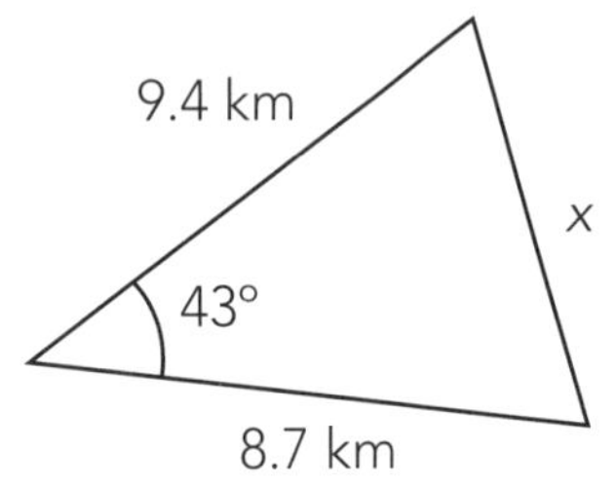

6

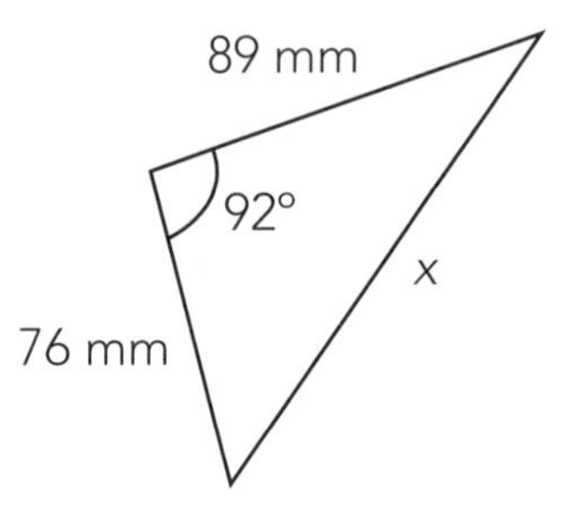

7

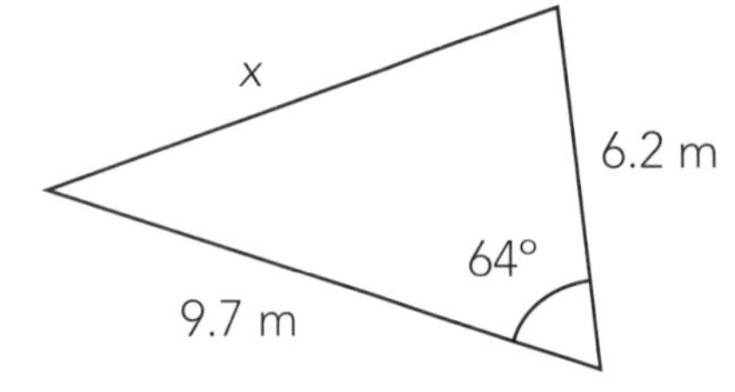

8

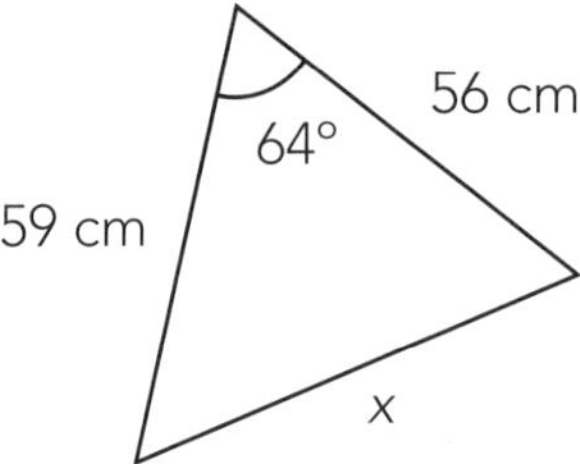

9

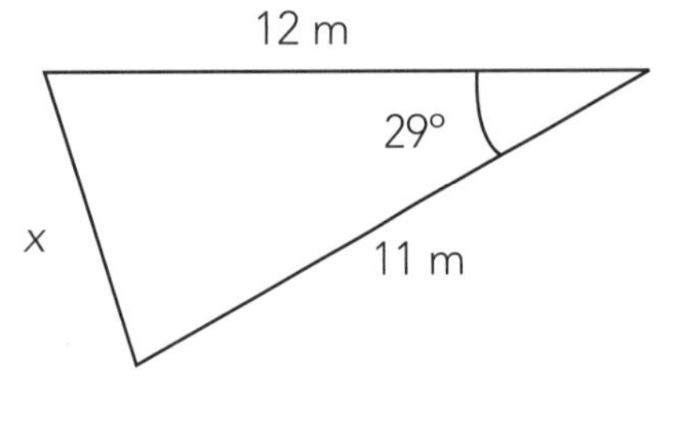

10

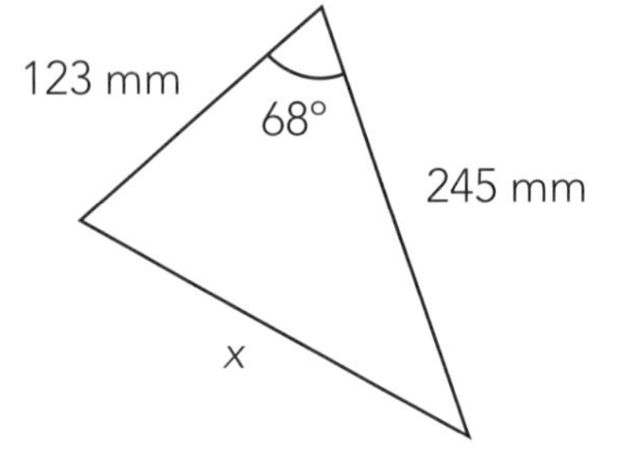

ISBN: 9780170354219

11

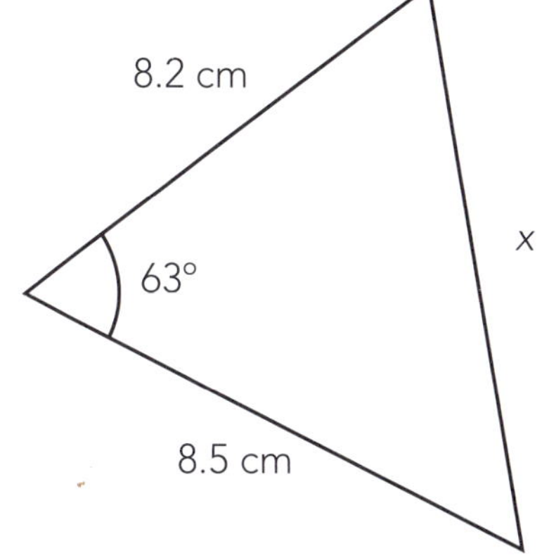

12

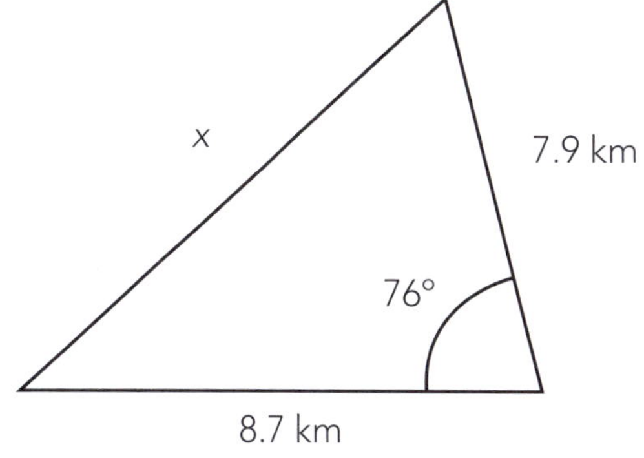

13

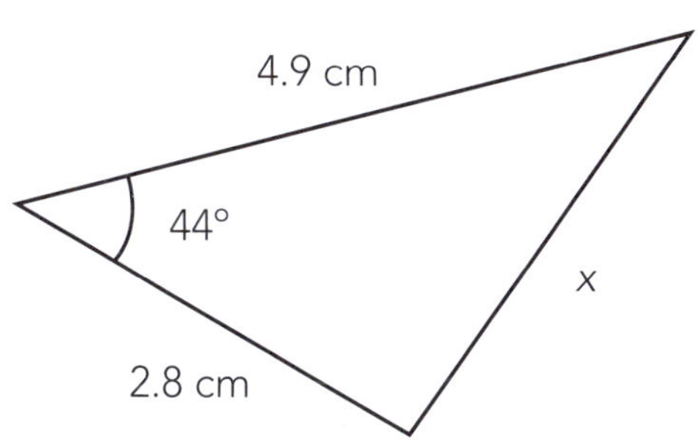

14

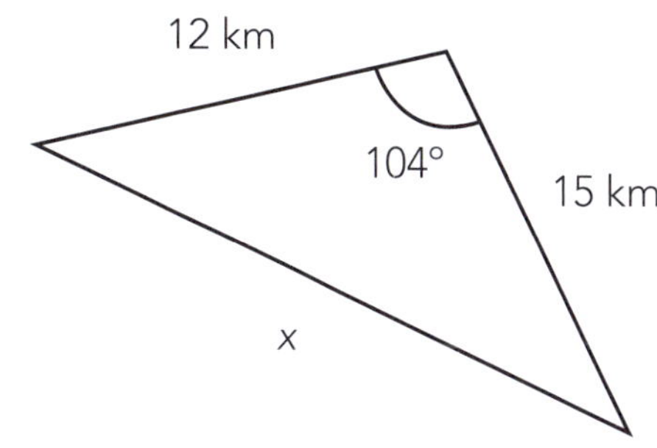

15

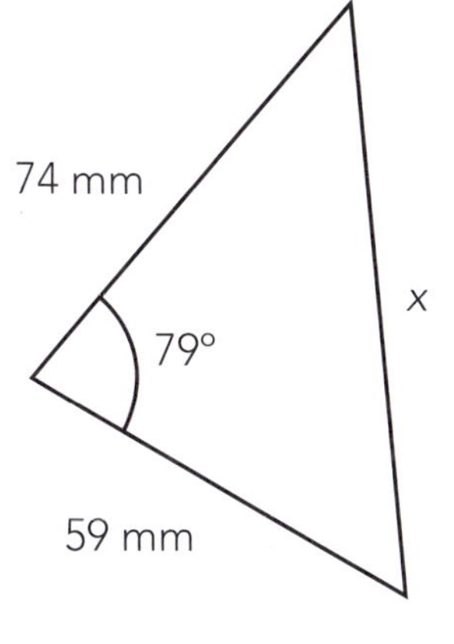

16

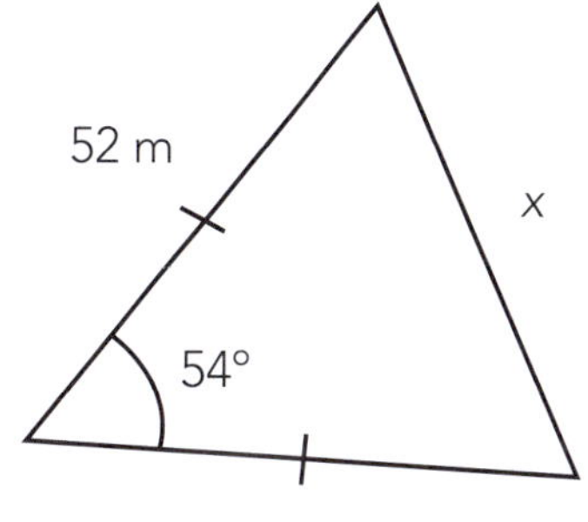

ISBN: 9780170354219

Cosine rule — finding angles

When we don't have opposites and need an angle, we use this form of the cosine rule:

$$\cos A = \frac{b^2 + c^2 - a^2}{2bc}$$

Example: Find the side *x*.

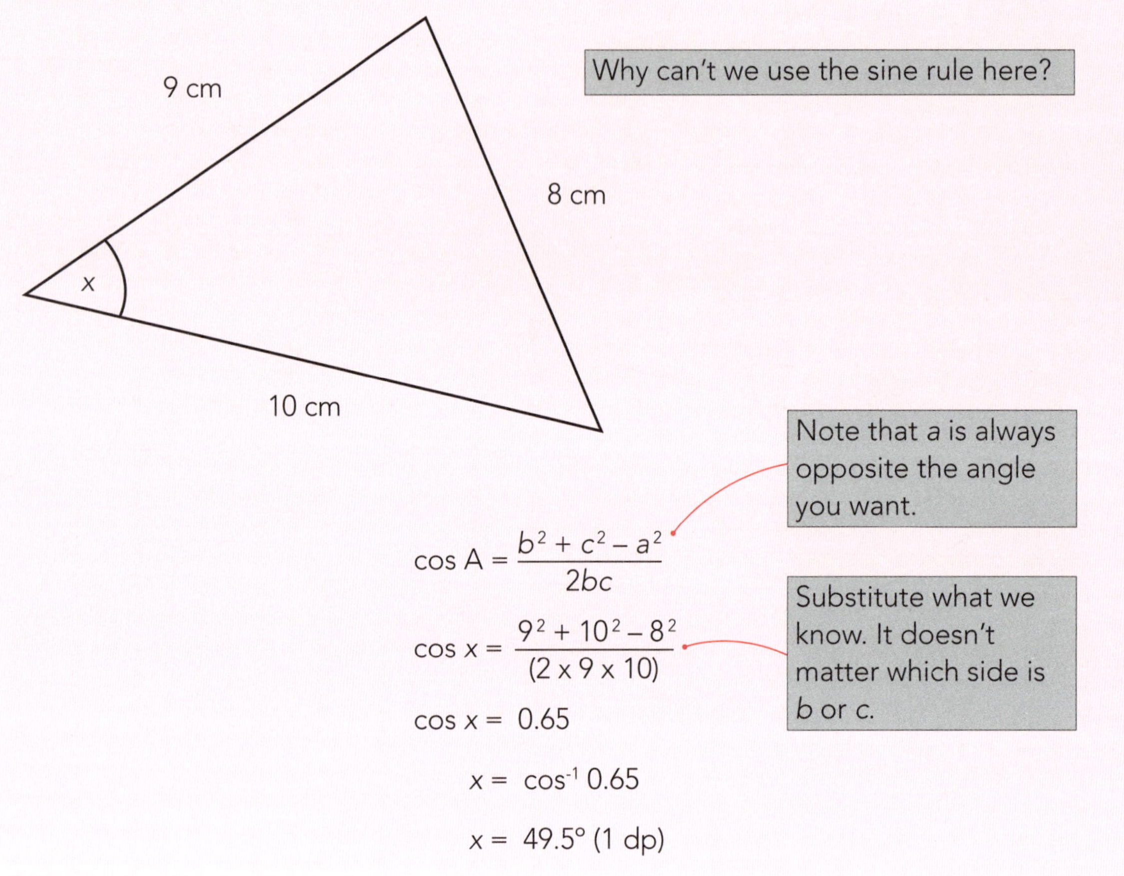

$$\cos A = \frac{b^2 + c^2 - a^2}{2bc}$$

$$\cos x = \frac{9^2 + 10^2 - 8^2}{(2 \times 9 \times 10)}$$

$$\cos x = 0.65$$

$$x = \cos^{-1} 0.65$$

$$x = 49.5° \text{ (1 dp)}$$

Find the marked angles of these triangles.

1

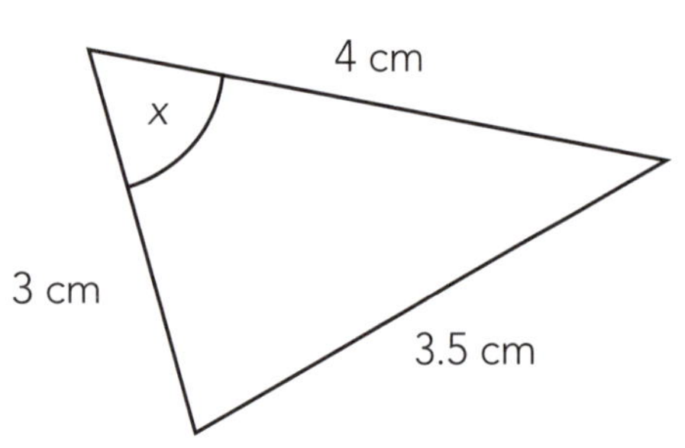

2

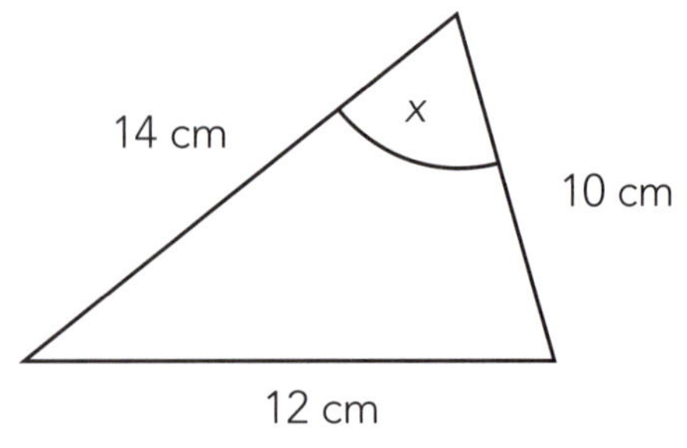

ISBN: 9780170354219

3

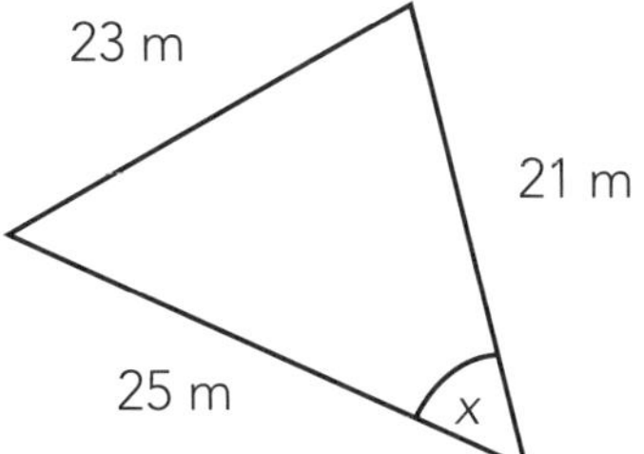

4

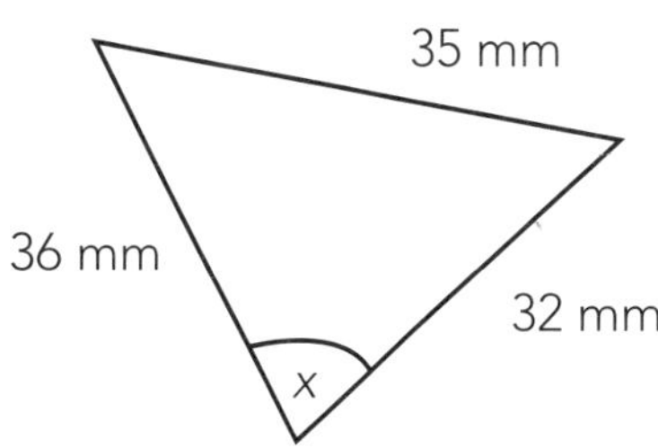

5

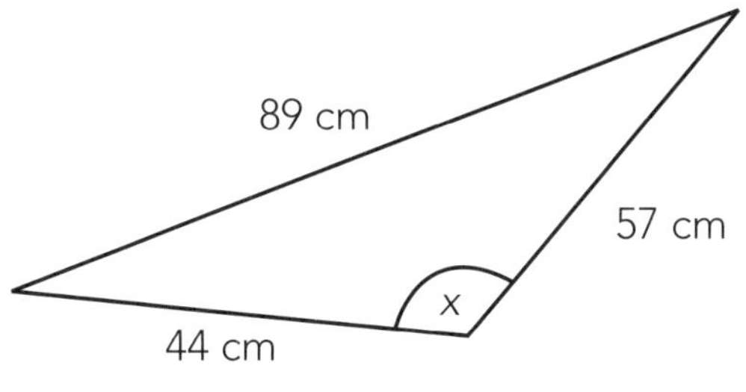

6

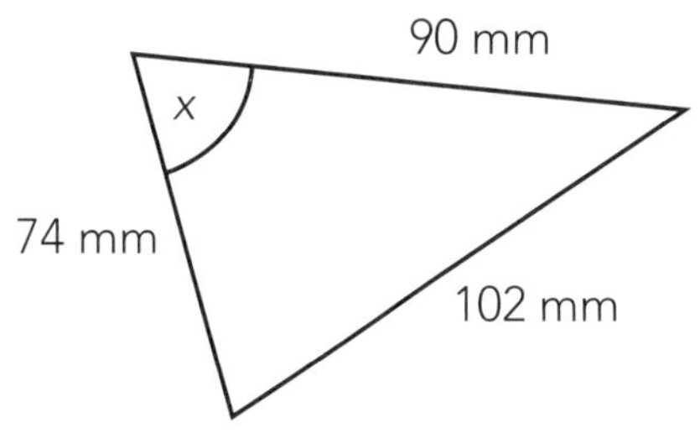

7

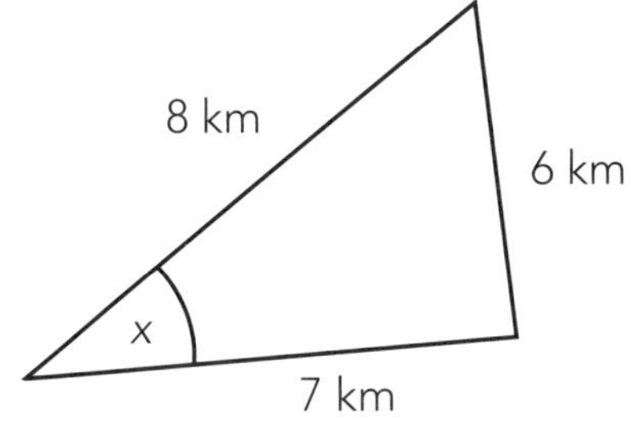

8

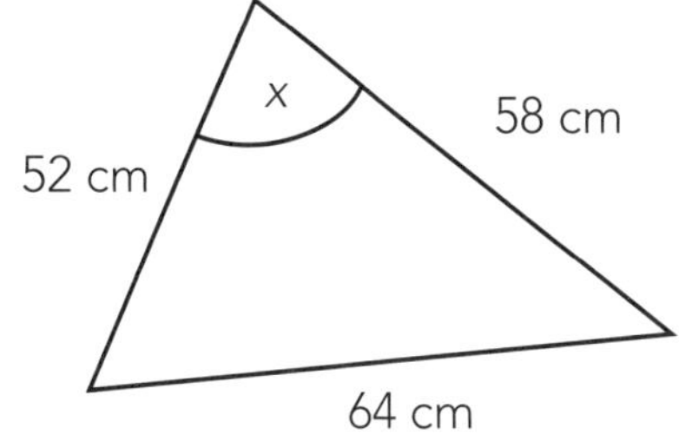

9

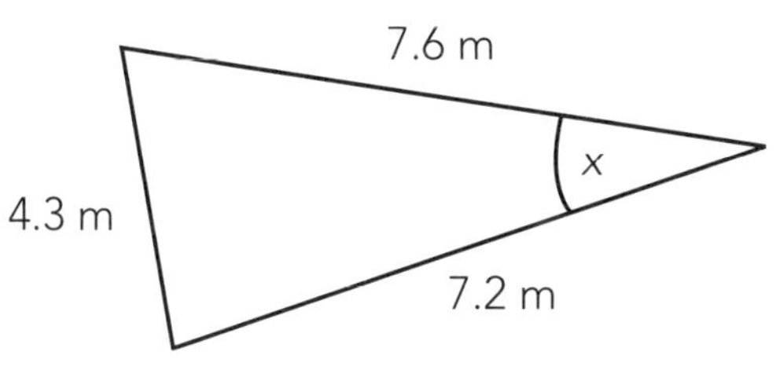

10

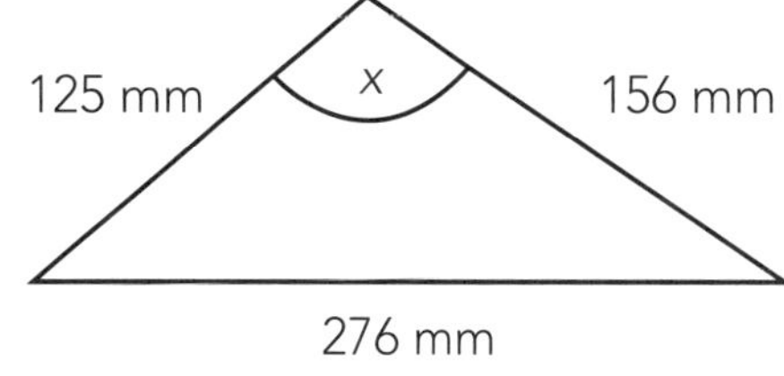

ISBN: 9780170354219

11

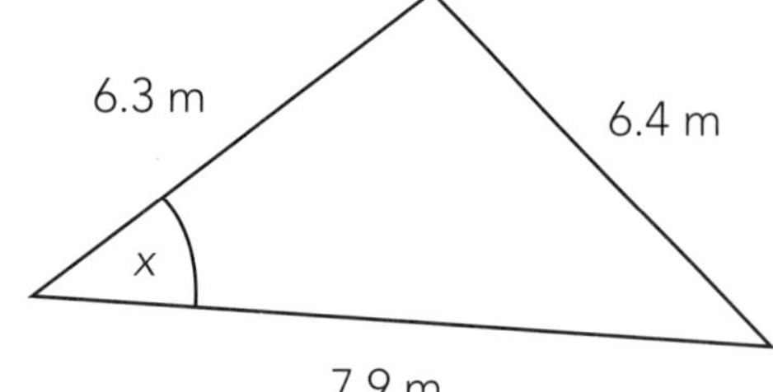

12

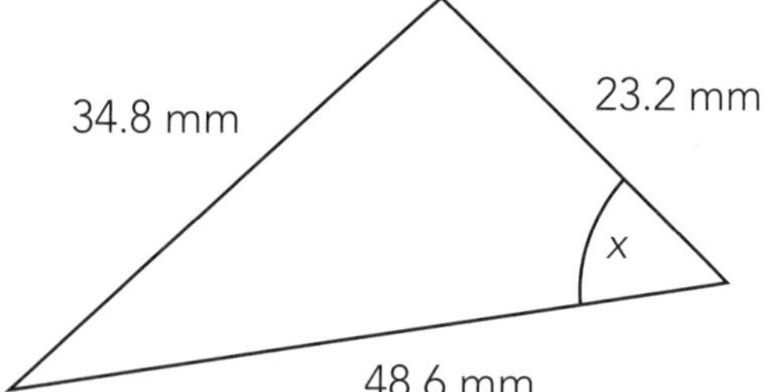

13

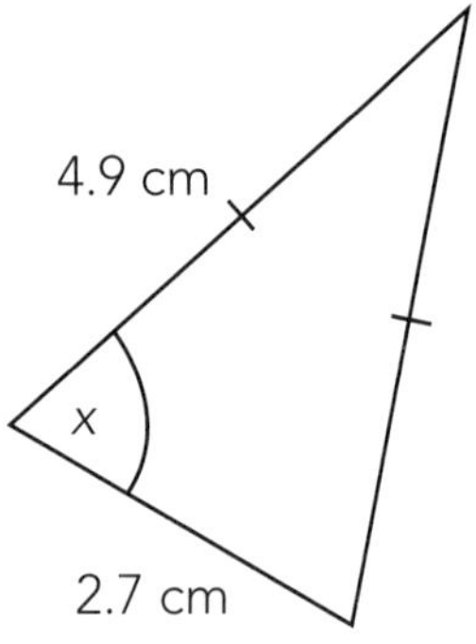

14

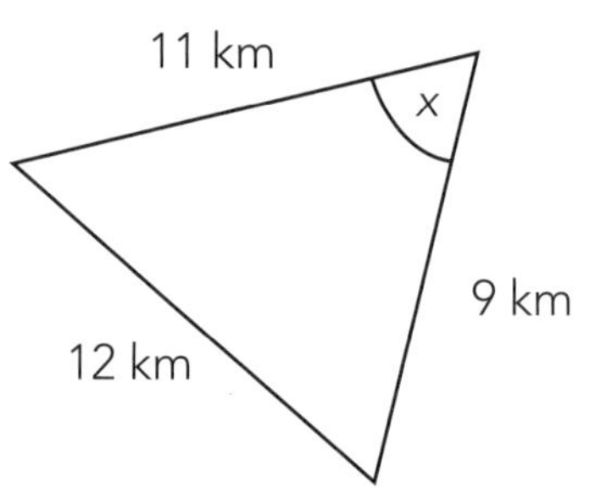

15 Find the smallest angle.

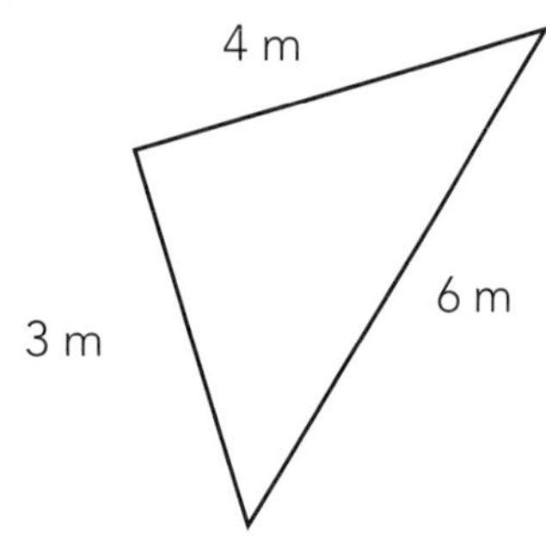

16 Find the largest angle.

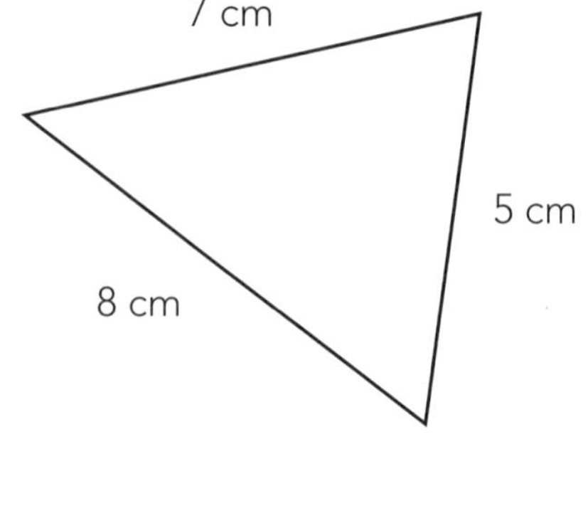

ISBN: 9780170354219

Which formula to use?

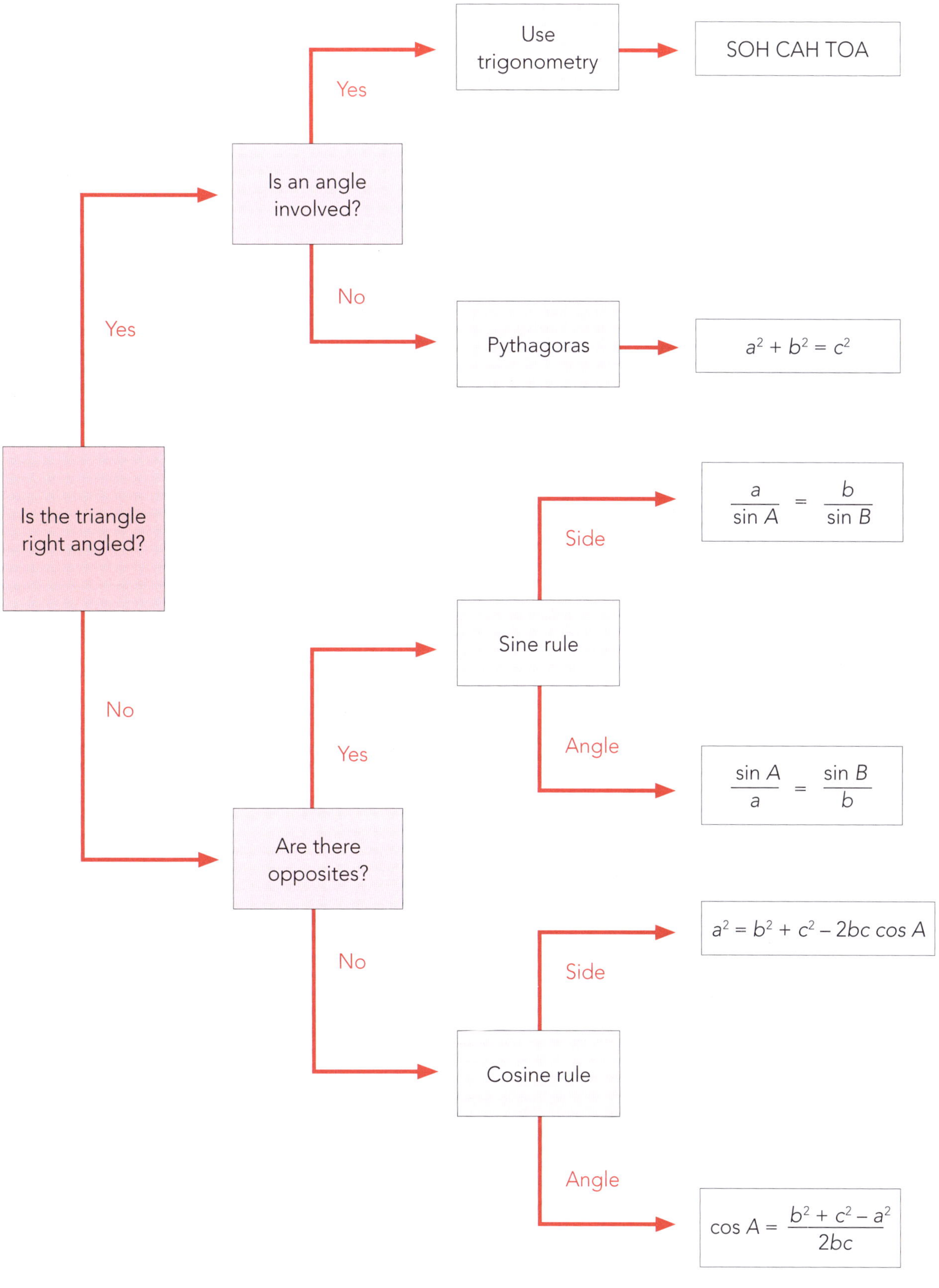

ISBN: 9780170354219

Putting it together

Now you will have to choose the correct formula to use to find the missing sides or angles.

Remember:

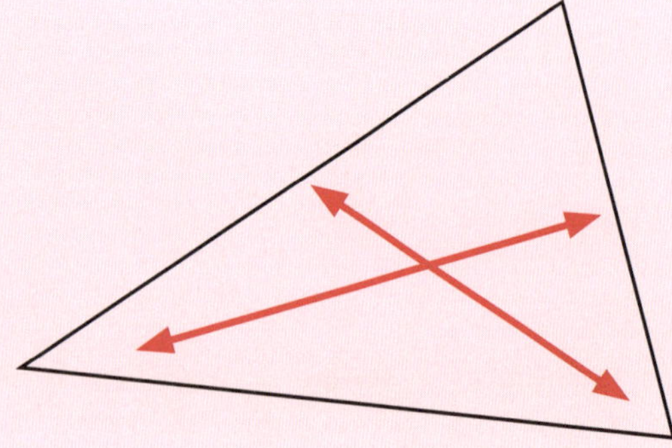

If you have opposites, use the sine rule.

Whatever you are trying to find goes on top.

If you don't have opposites, and there is no right angle, then use one of the cosine rules. Make sure you identify what you are trying to find.

Use the appropriate formula to find these missing sides and angles.

1

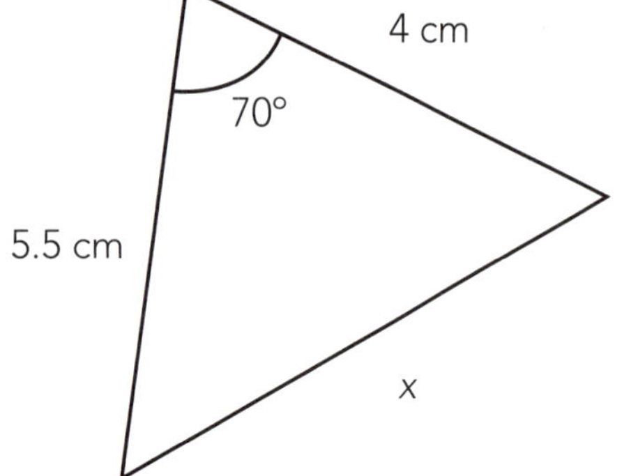

2

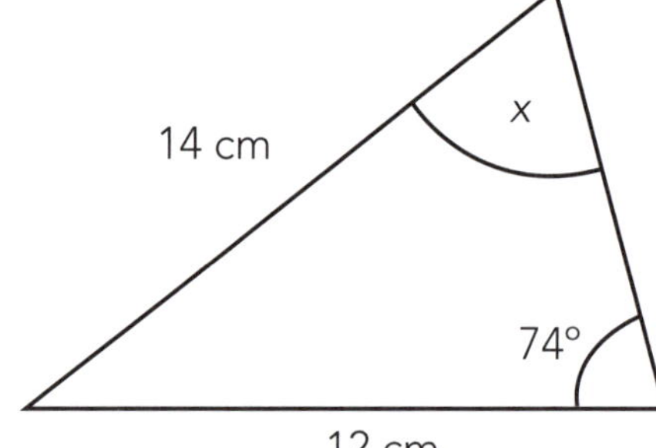

 ISBN: 9780170354219

3

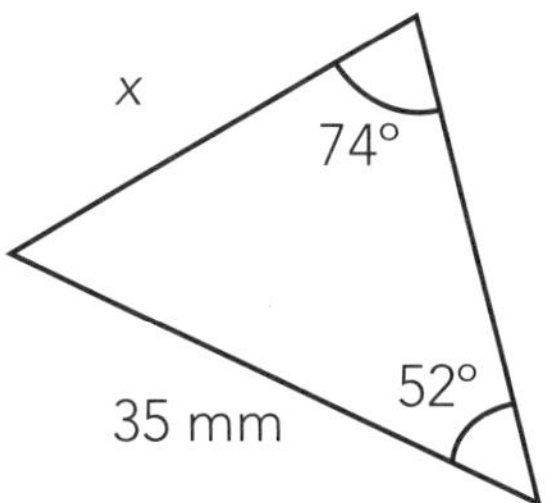

4

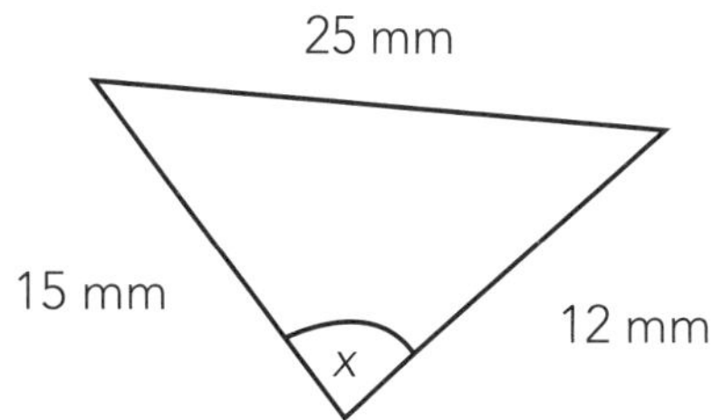

5

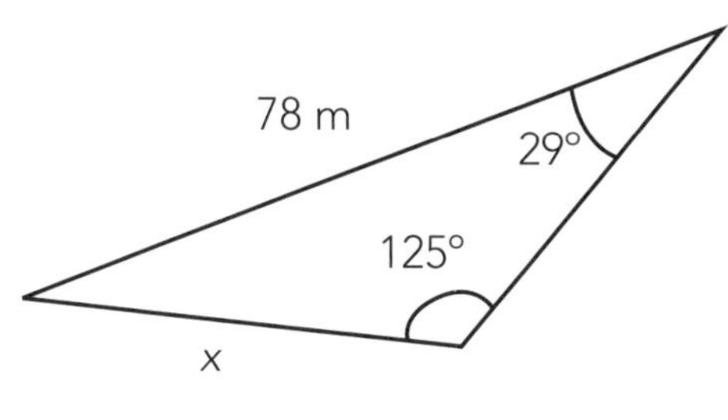

6

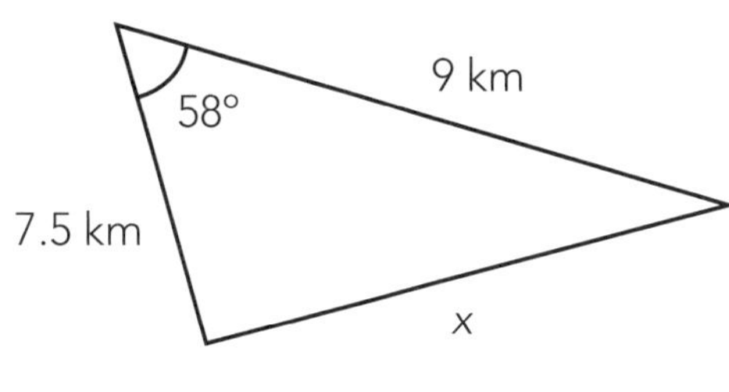

7

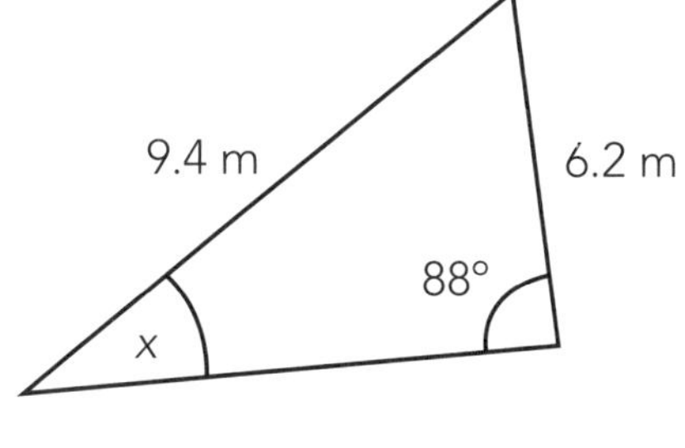

8

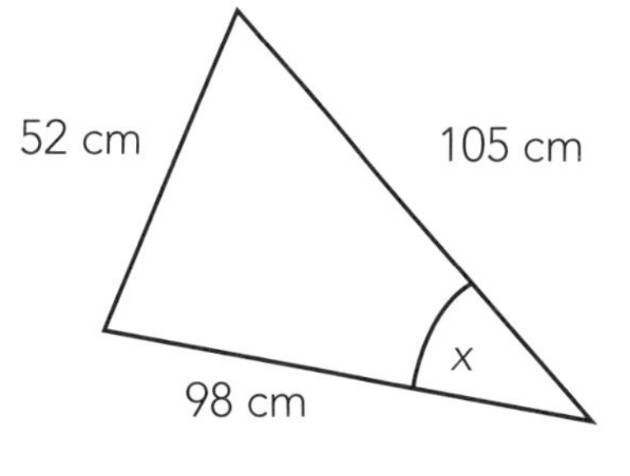

9

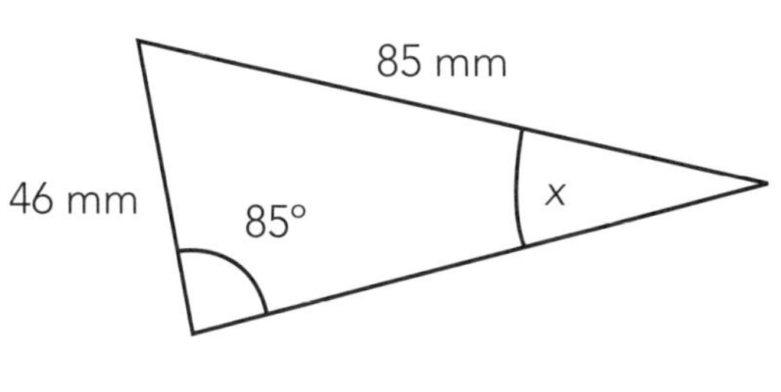

10

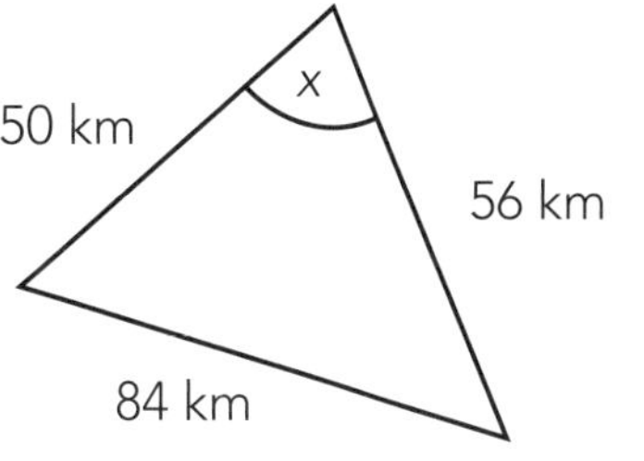

ISBN: 9780170354219

11

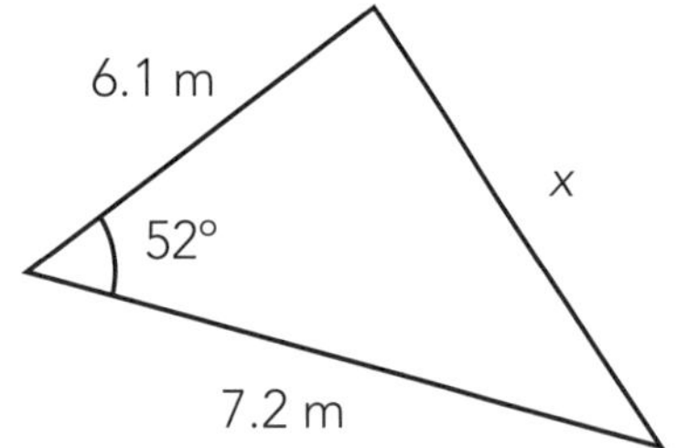

12

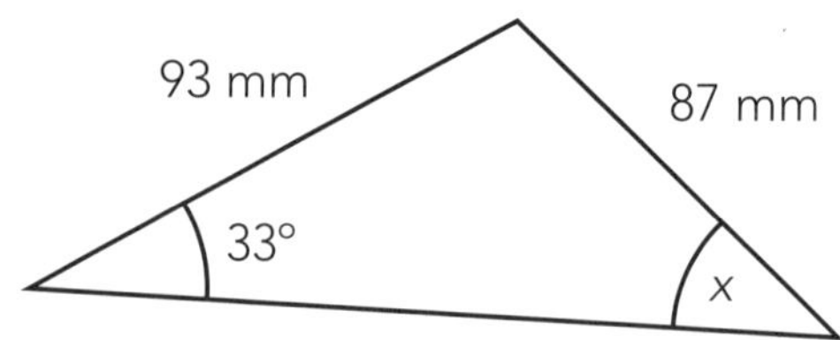

13

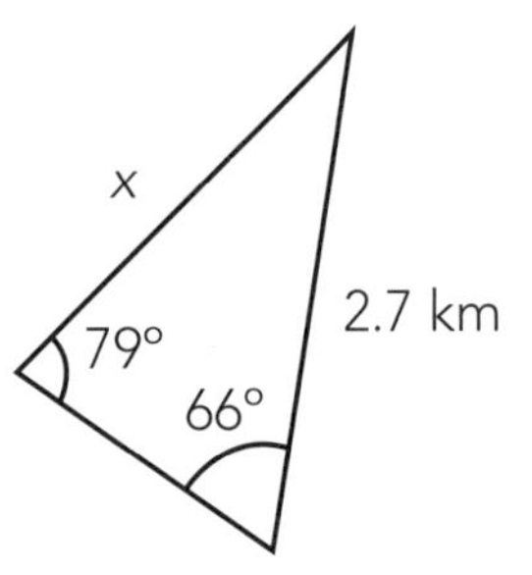

14

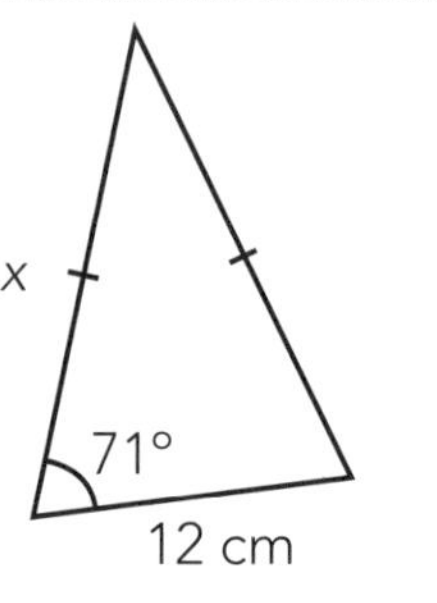

15

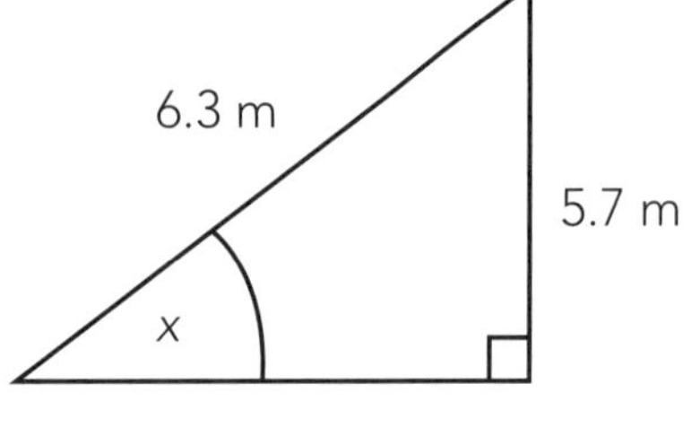

16

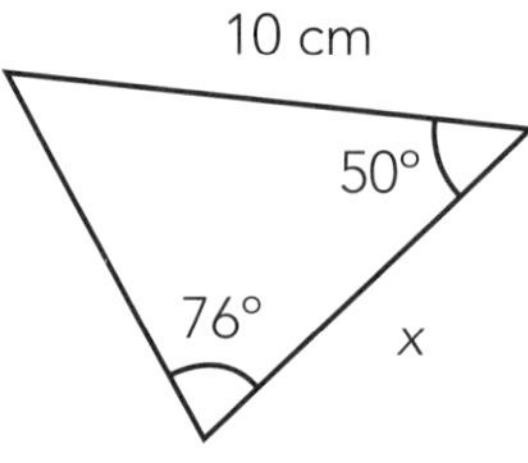

17

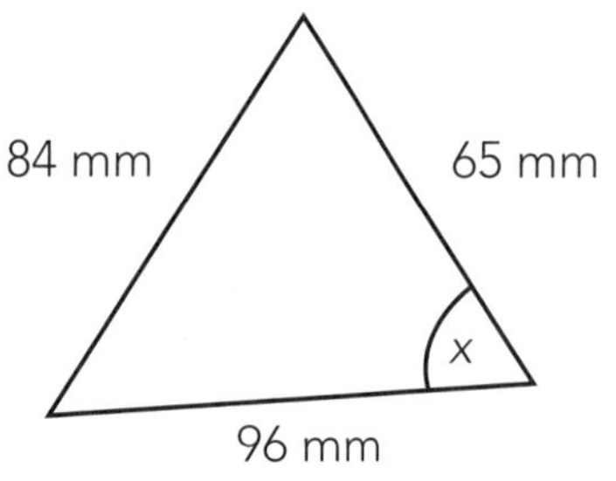

18

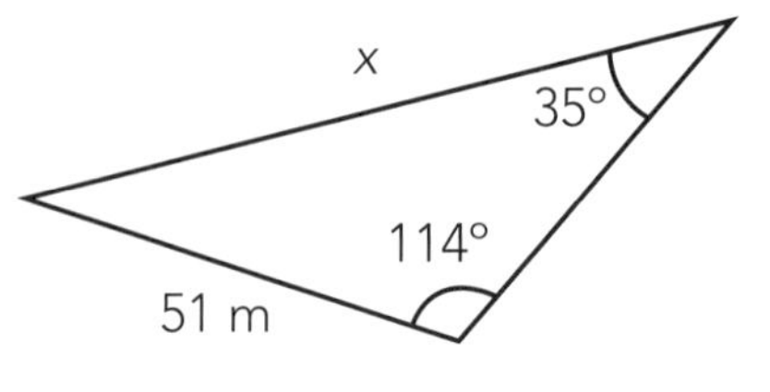

ISBN: 9780170354219

19 ABCD is a parallelogram.

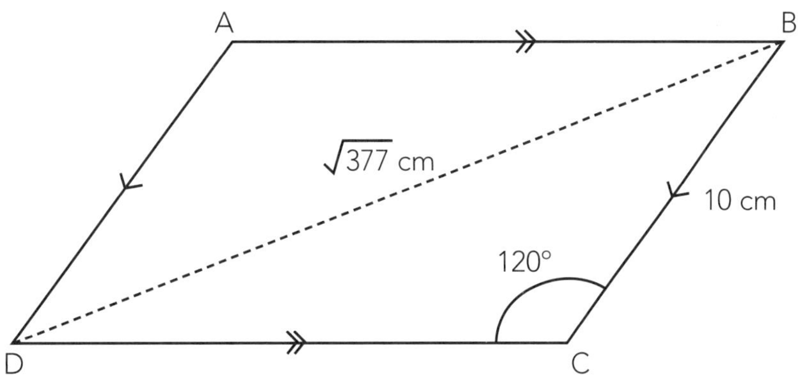

a Calculate the length of AB.

b Calculate the length of the short diagonal (AC).

20 Calculate the vertical height of this triangle (h).

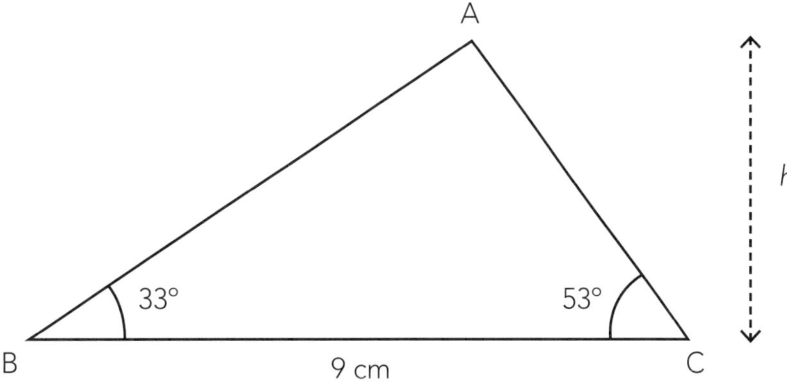

ISBN: 9780170354219

21 Angle BAD is 98°. Find the length of BC.

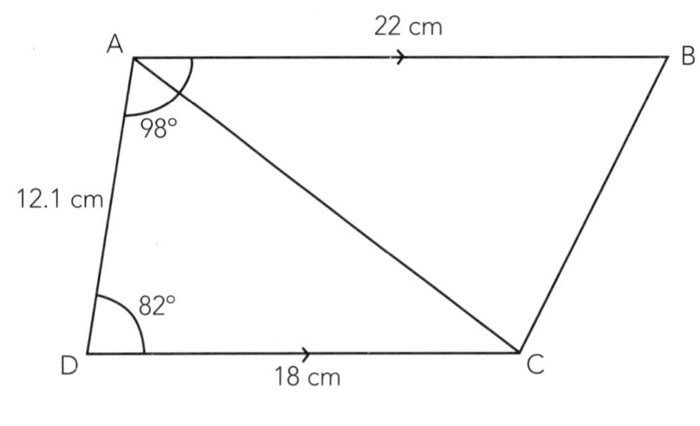

22 Chloe would like to know the width of a river. She is able to measure the angle of elevation from the top of the 2 m high bank where she is standing (22°). She then moves to a point 50 m from the bank and again measures the angle of elevation (15°). Use this information to do the following.

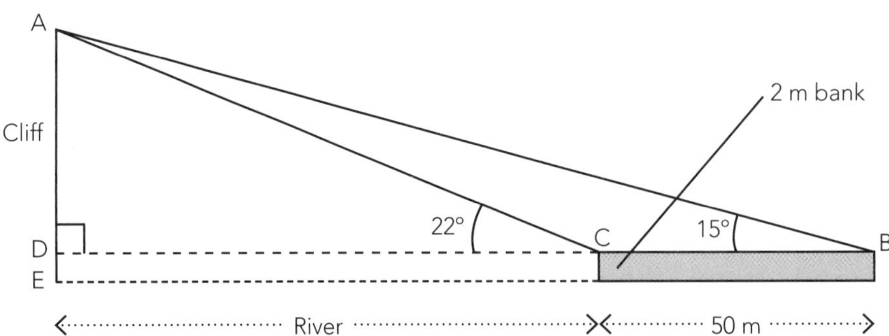

a Calculate the total height of the cliff (AE).

b Calculate the width of the river (DC).

 ISBN: 9780170354219

Areas

Triangles, other polygons and circles

Find the area of these shapes.

1

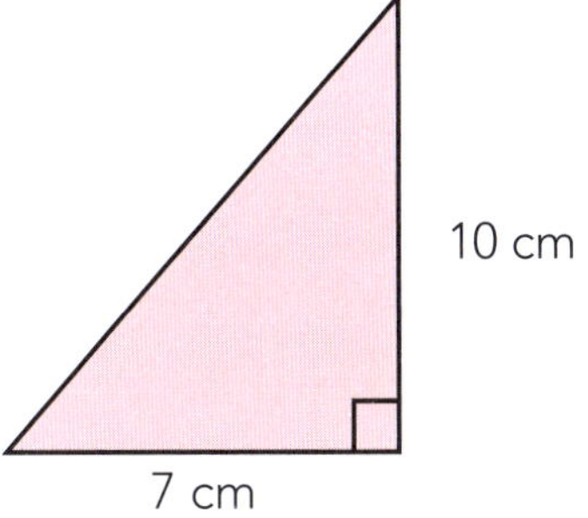

2

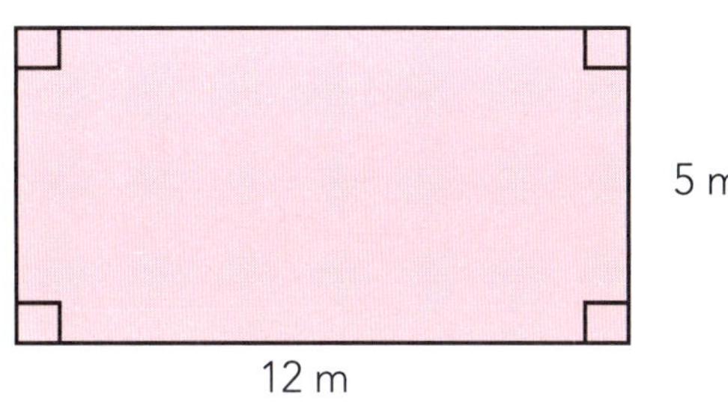

3

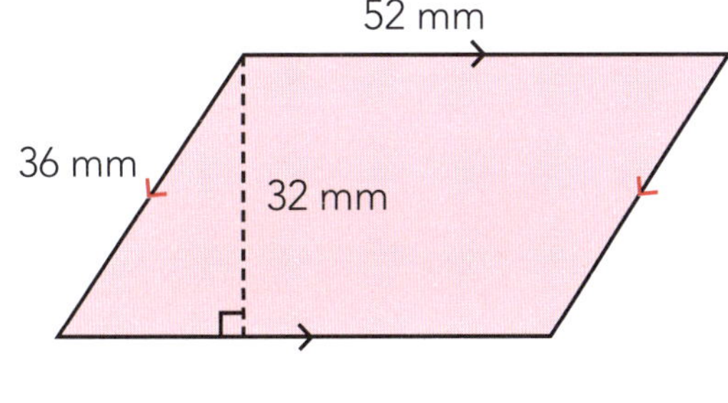

4

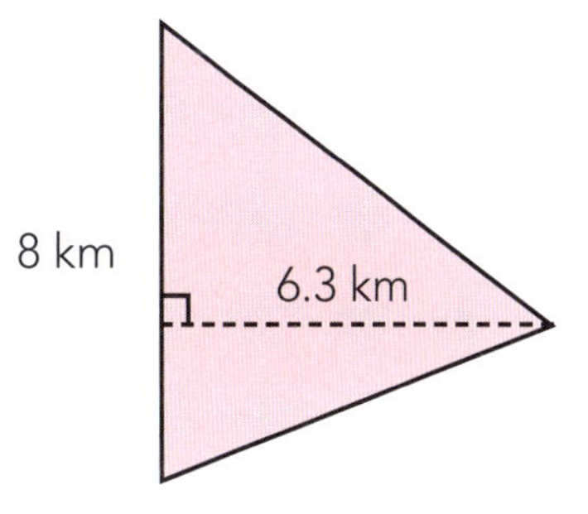

5

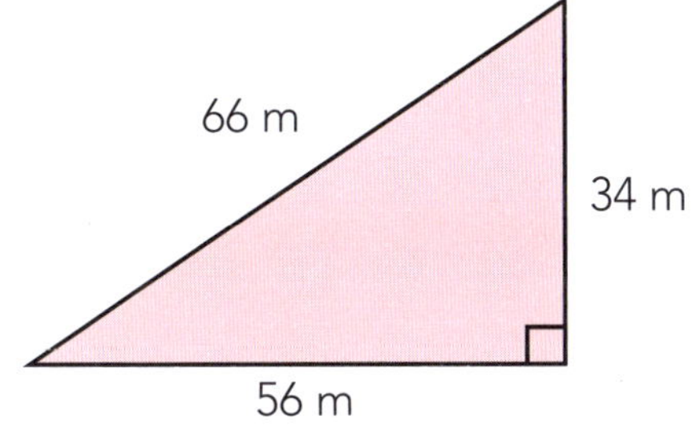

6

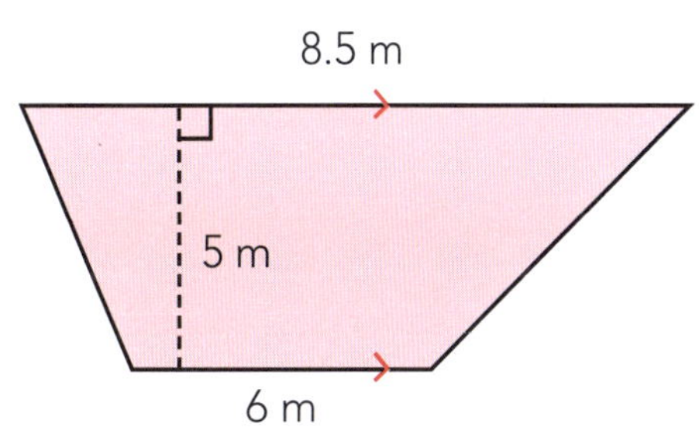

ISBN: 9780170354219

7

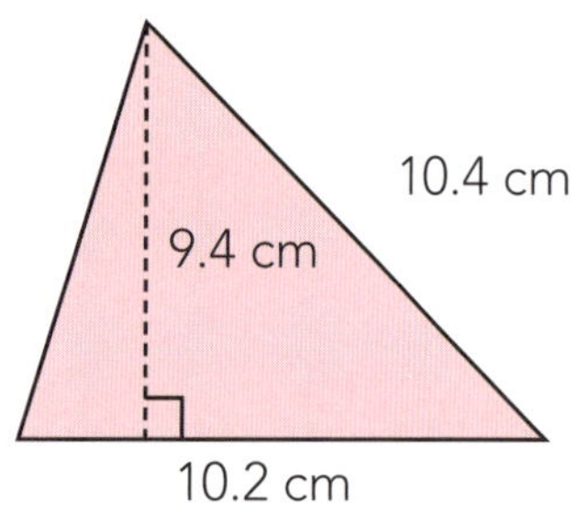

8

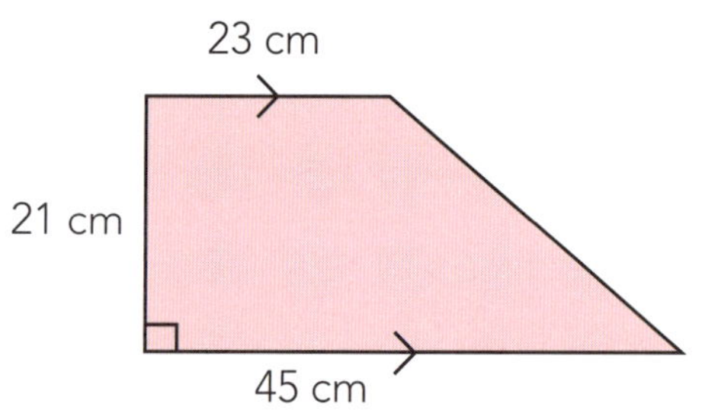

9

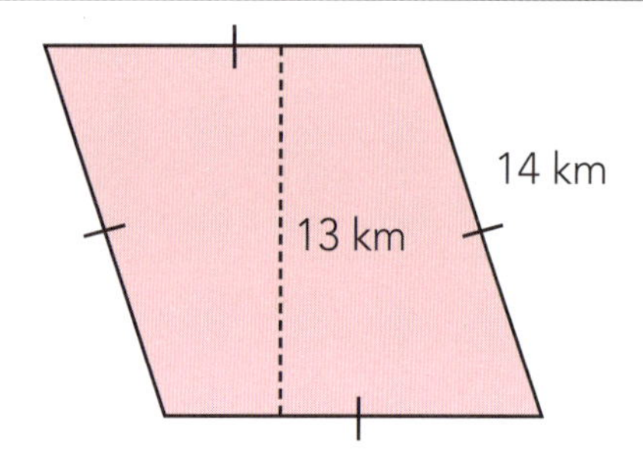

10

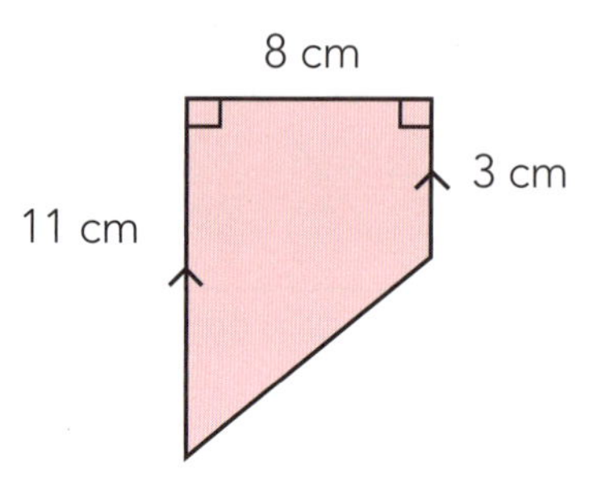

11

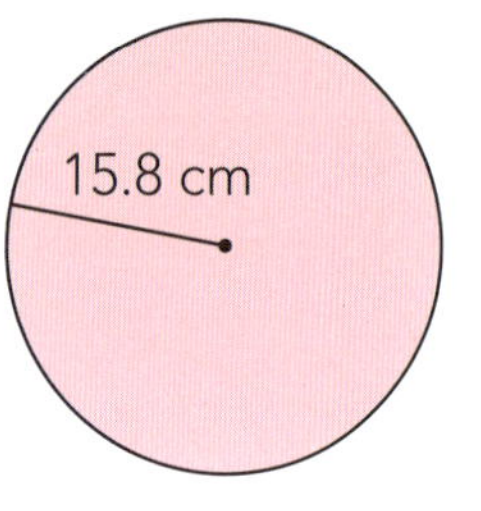

12

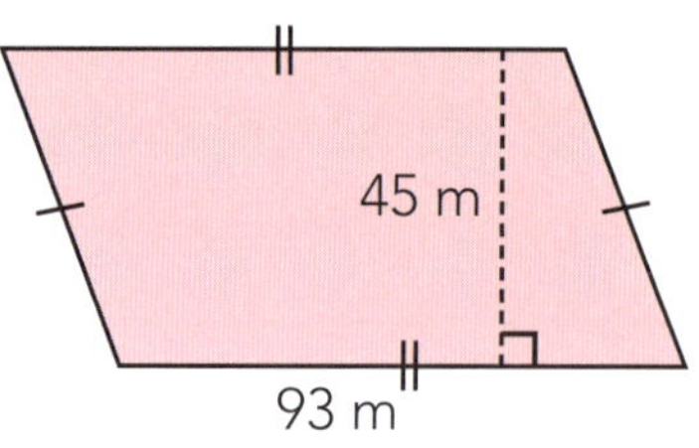

13

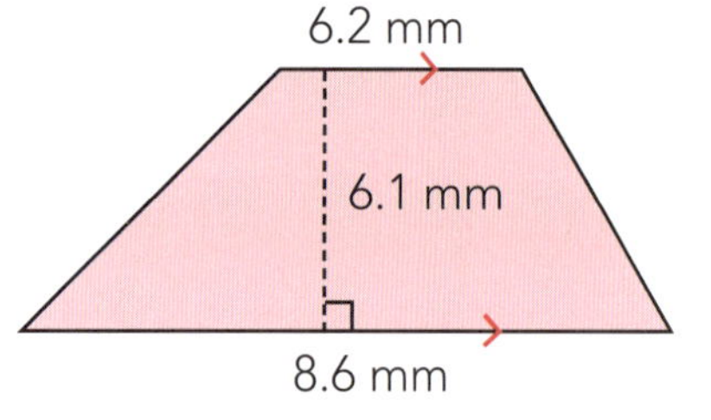

14

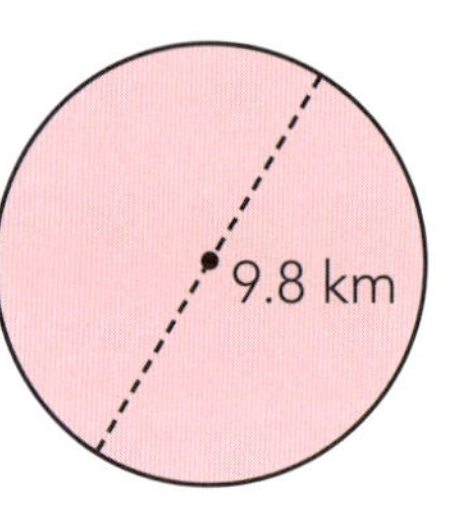

 ISBN: 9780170354219

15 This figure is a quarter circle with a circle cut out of it.

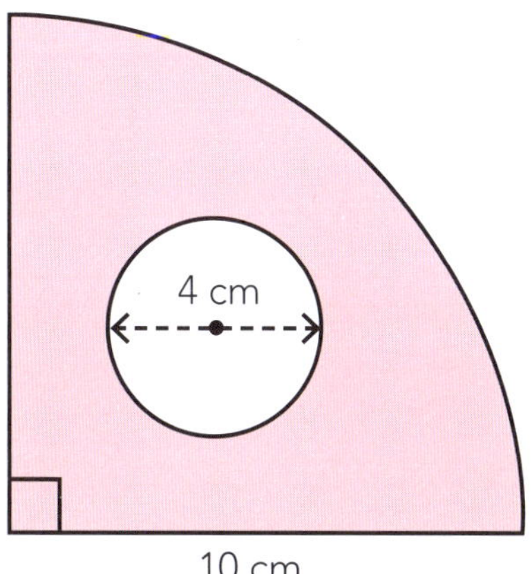

16 This figure is a parallelogram with a square cut out of it.

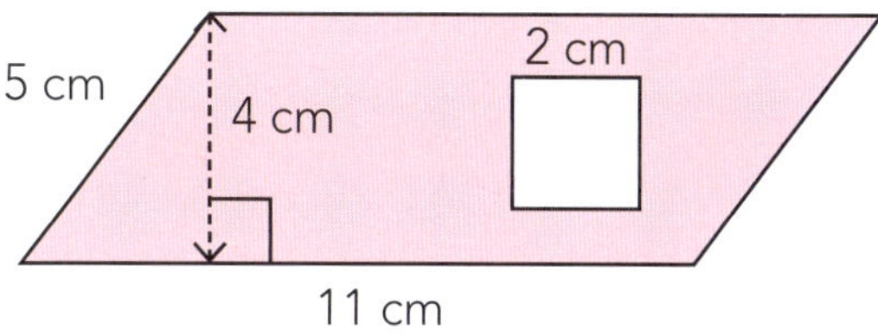

17 This figure is an isosceles triangle with a semicircle cut out of it.

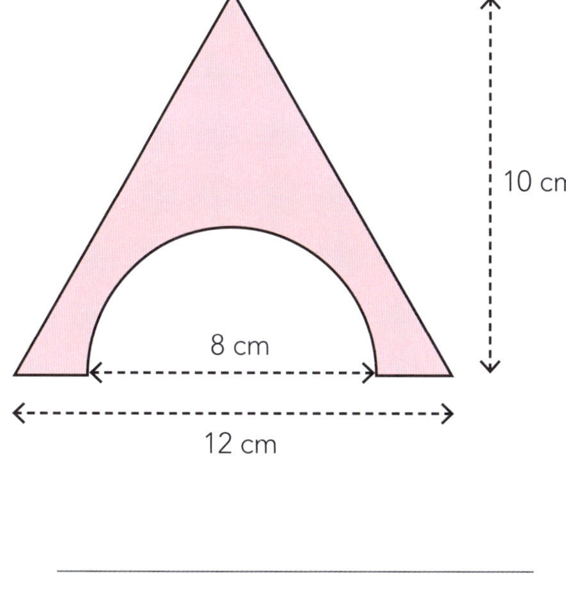

18 This area is a trapezium with a quarter circle cut out of it.

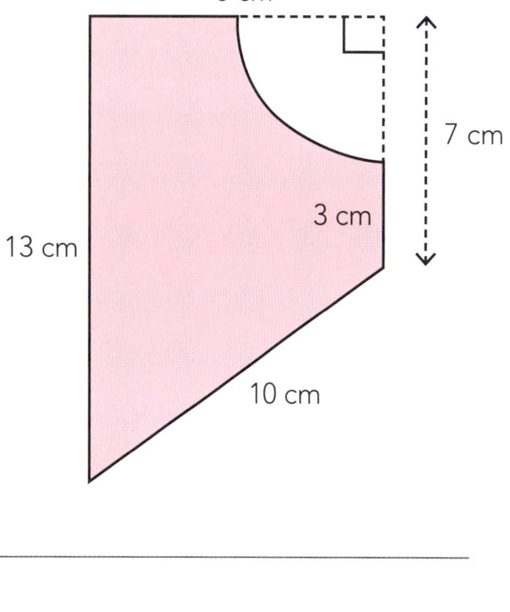

19 This figure is a triangle with a parallelogram cut out of it.

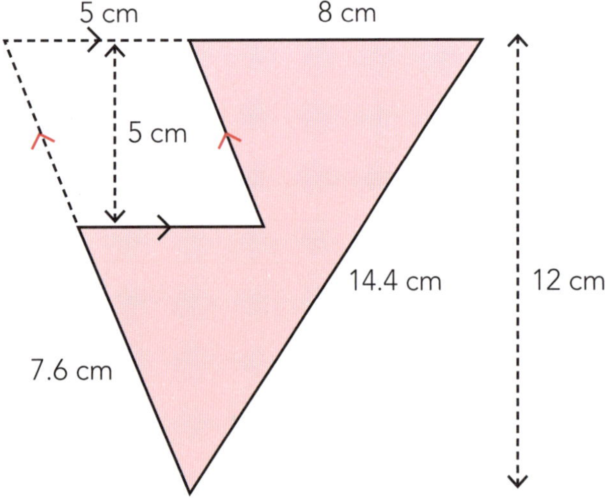

20 This figure is constructed using semicircles and lines.

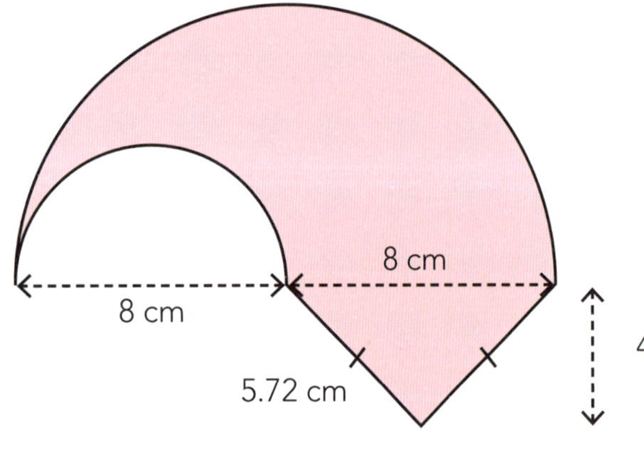

ISBN: 9780170354219

Non-right-angled triangles

You may also be required to find the area of a non-right-angled triangle. This is the formula to use:

$$\text{Area} = \frac{1}{2}bc\sin A$$

Example: Find the area of the triangle.

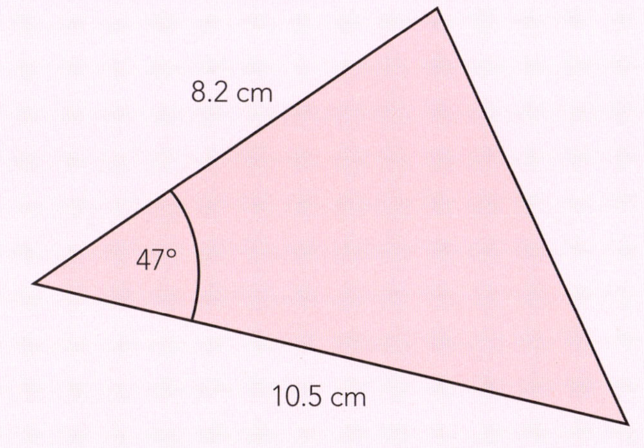

Notice that we use the two sides and the angle between.

$$\text{Area} = \frac{1}{2}bc\sin A$$

$$\text{Area} = \frac{1}{2} \times 8.2 \times 10.5 \times \sin 47°$$

$$\text{Area} = 31.48\text{ cm}^2\text{ (2 dp)}$$

Find the area of these triangles.

1

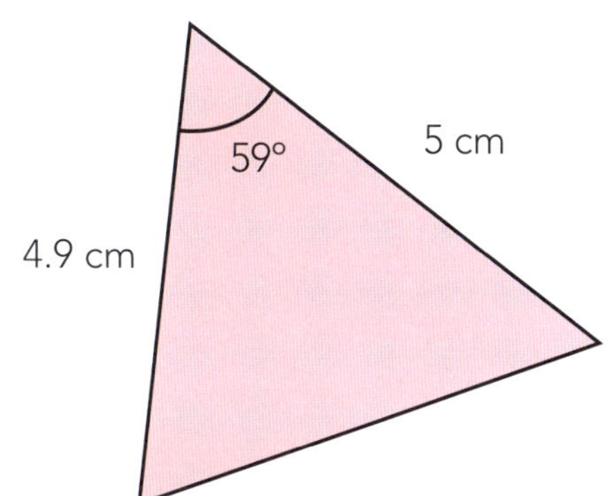

2

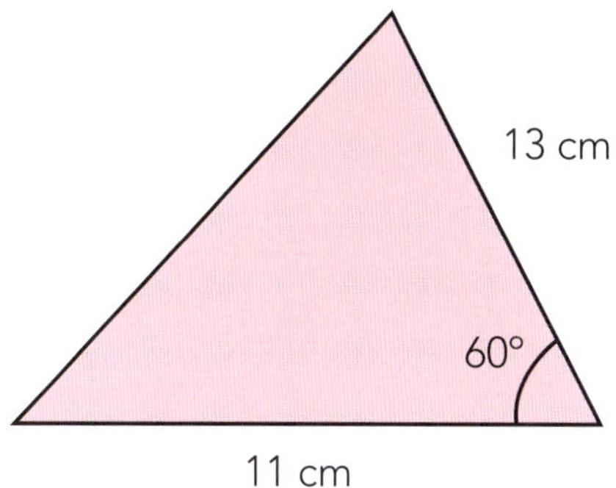

ISBN: 9780170354219

3

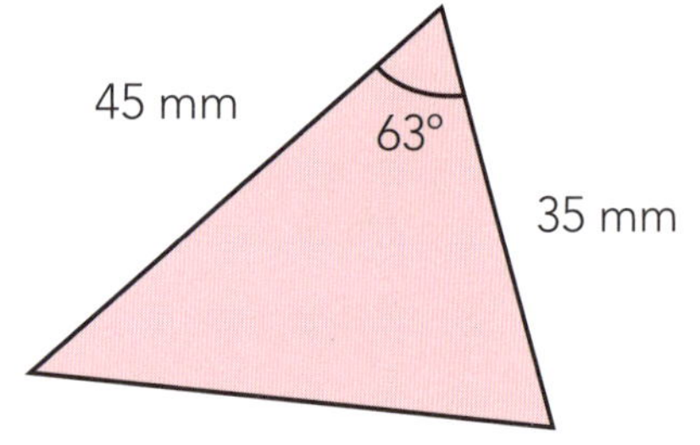

4

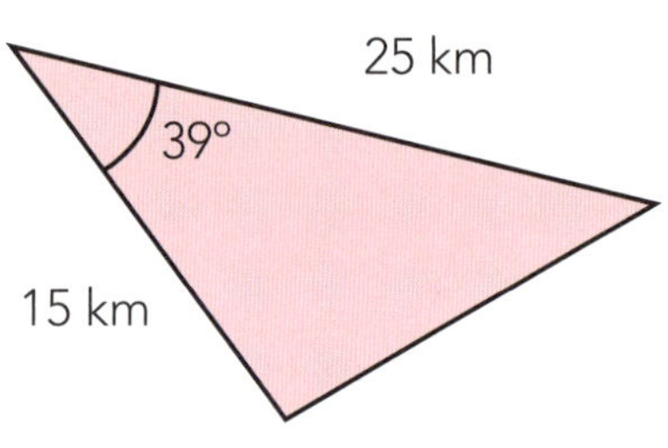

5

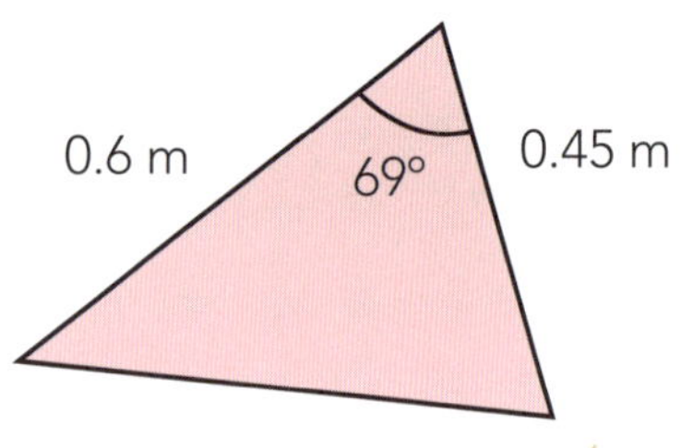

6

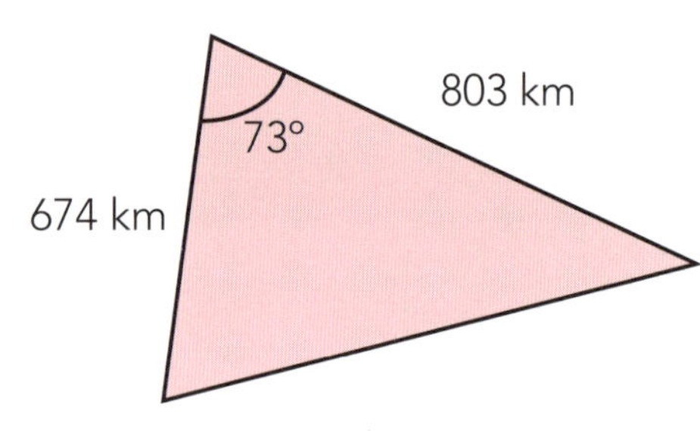

7

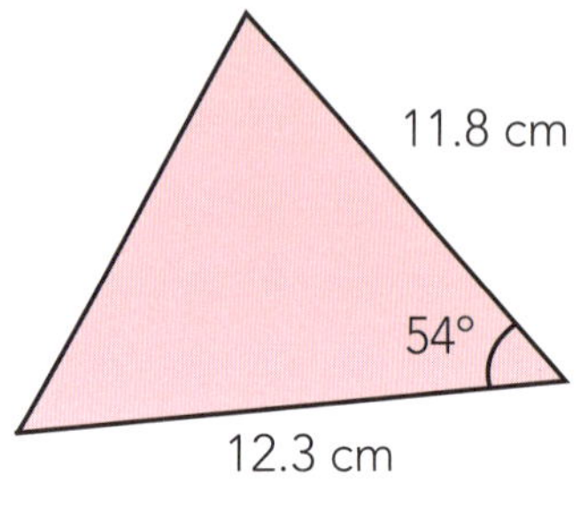

8

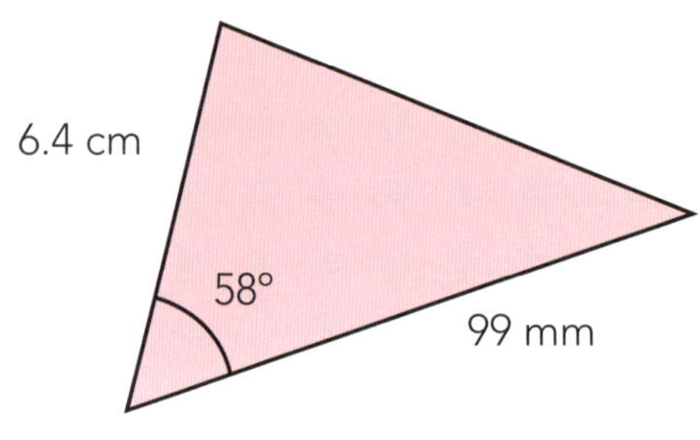

9

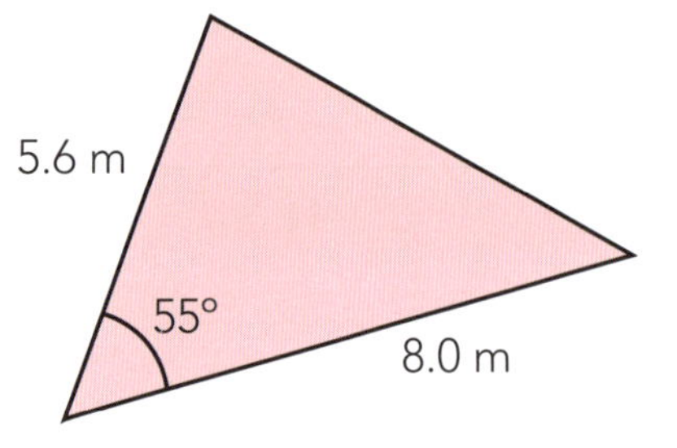

10

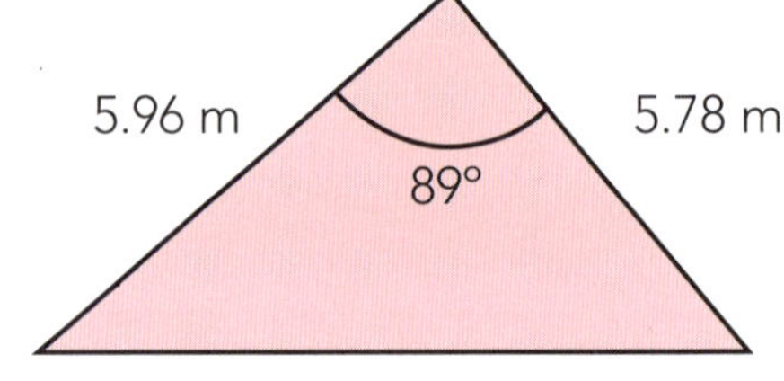

ISBN: 9780170354219

11

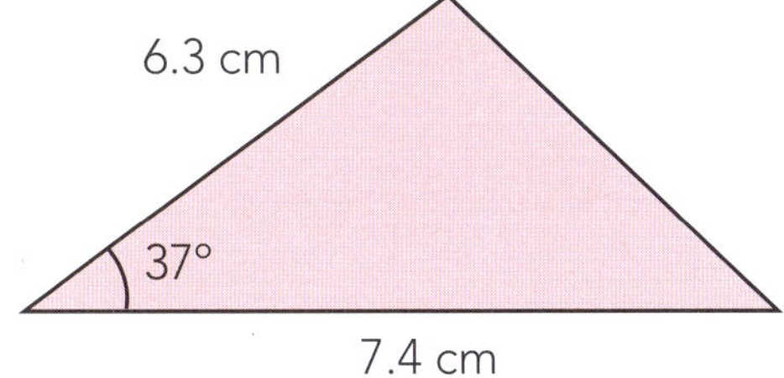

12

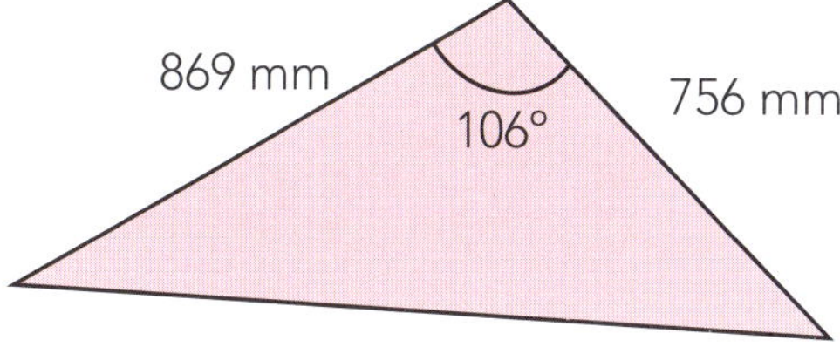

13

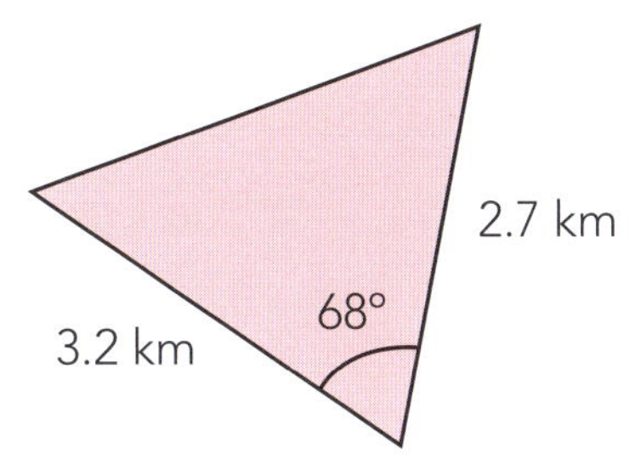

14

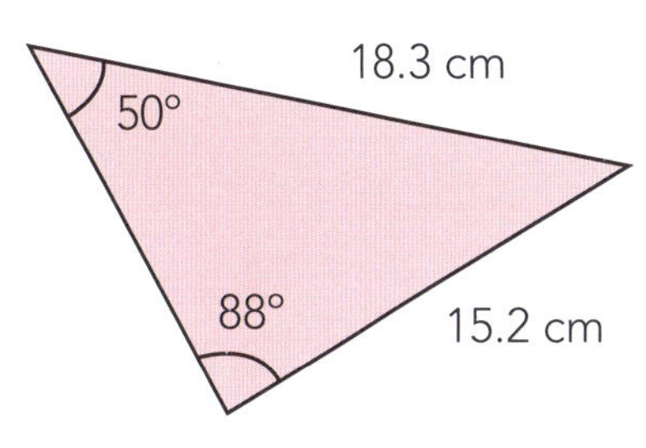

15

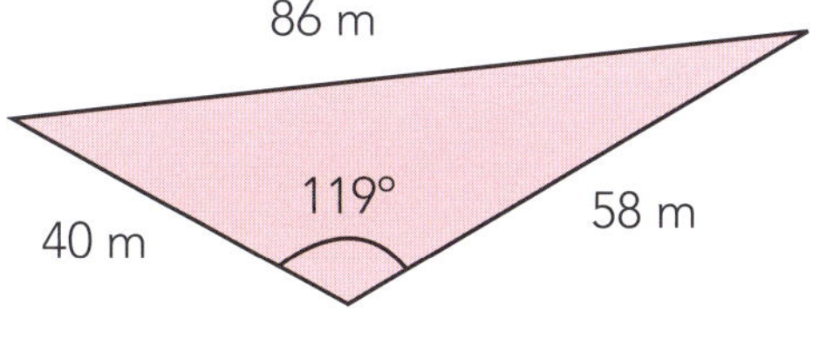

16

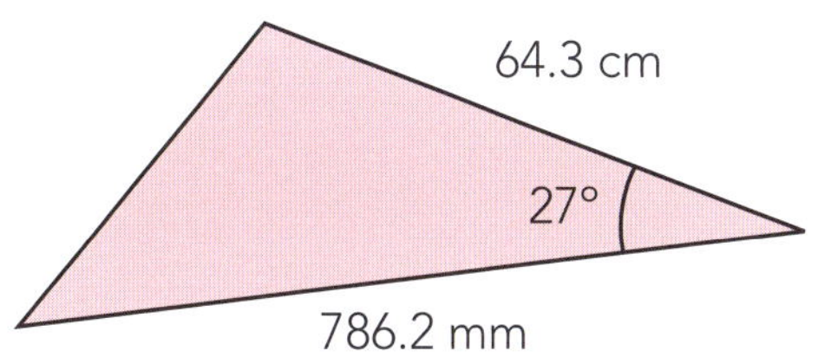

17

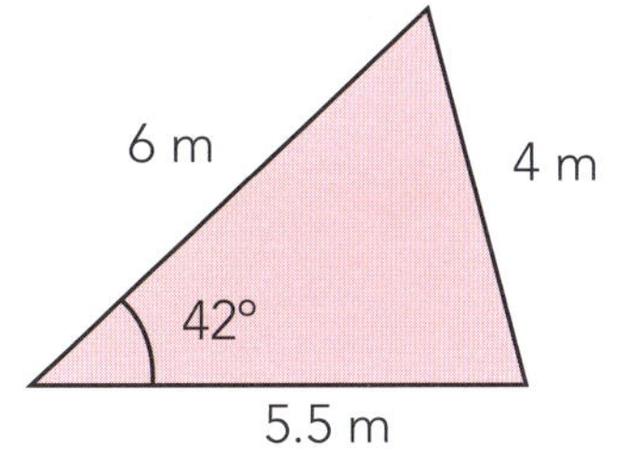

18

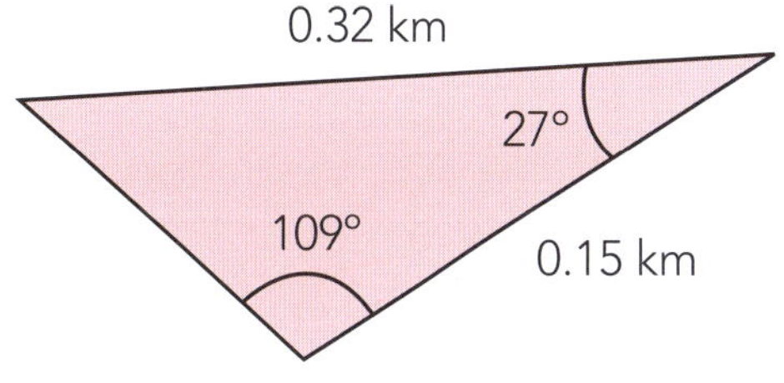

ISBN: 9780170354219

Circular measure

Arc length

You may also be required to find the length of an arc.
This is the formula to use:

$$\text{Arc length} = 2\pi r \frac{\theta}{360}$$

Example: Find the arc length (x).

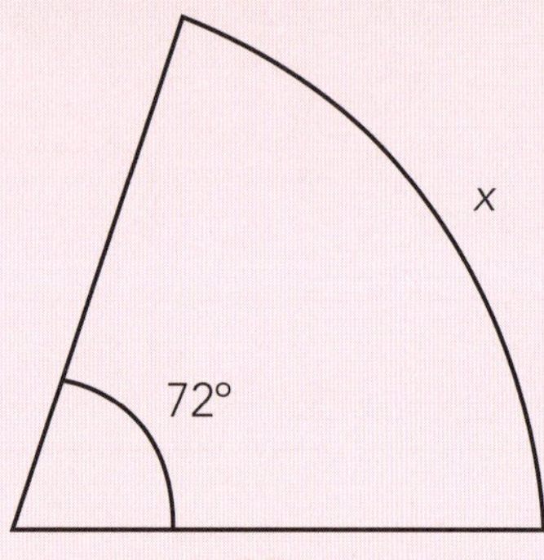

$$\text{Arc length} = 2\pi r \frac{\theta}{360}$$

$$\text{Arc length} = 2\pi \times 13.4 \times \frac{72}{360}$$

$$\text{Arc length} = 16.84 \text{ cm (2 dp)}$$

Find the following arc lengths.

1

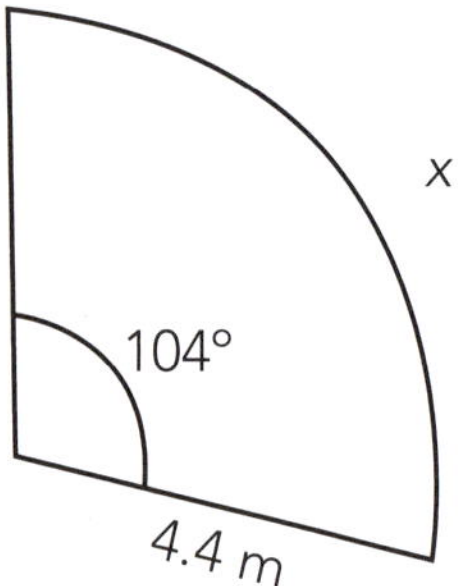

2

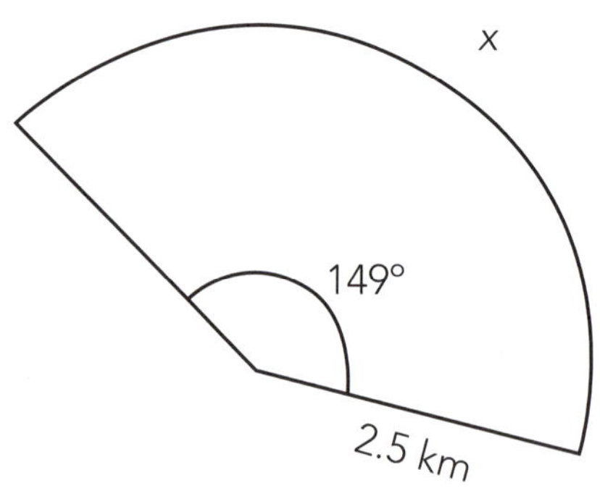

ISBN: 9780170354219

3

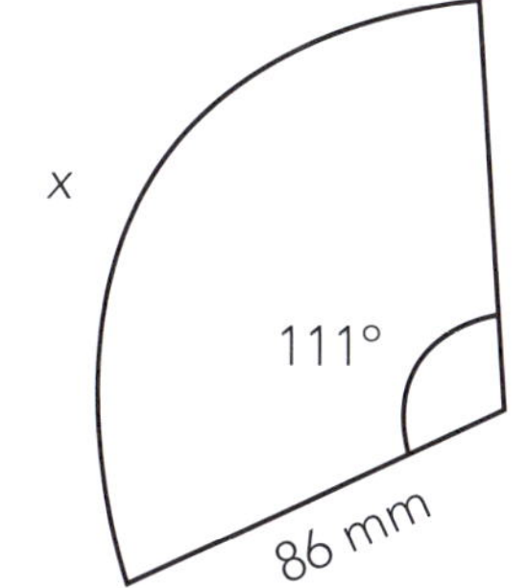

4

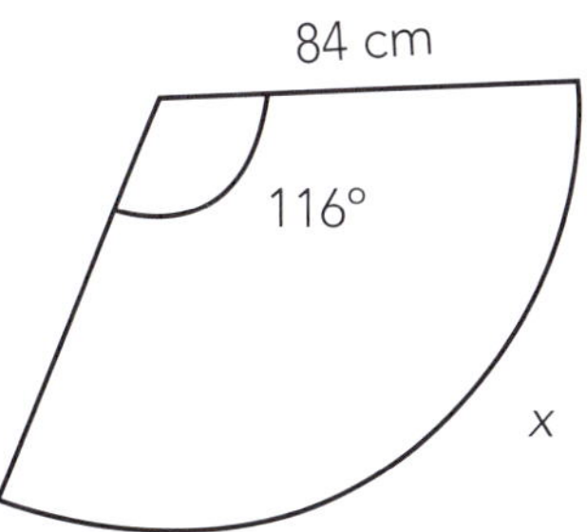

5

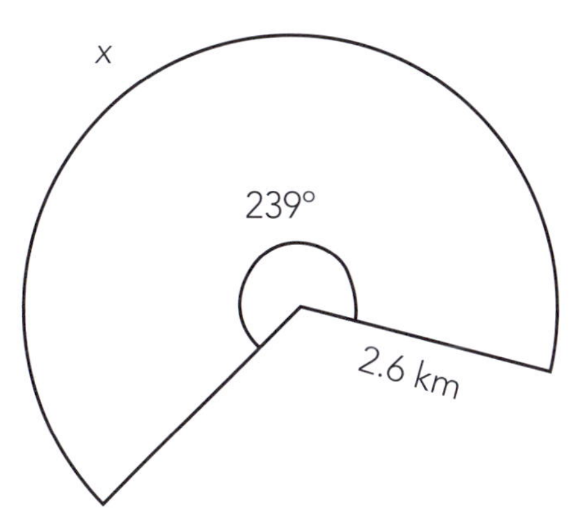

6

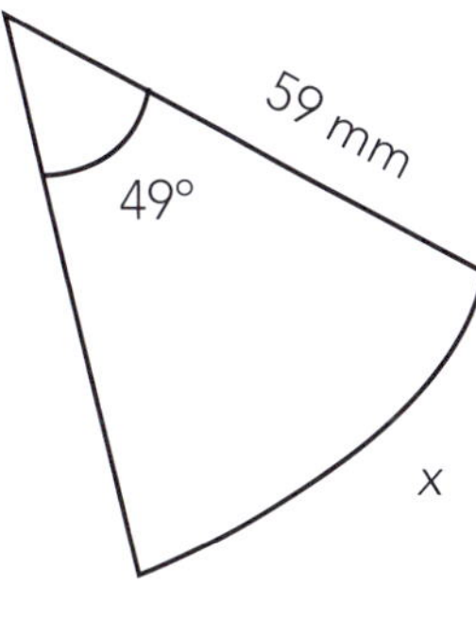

7

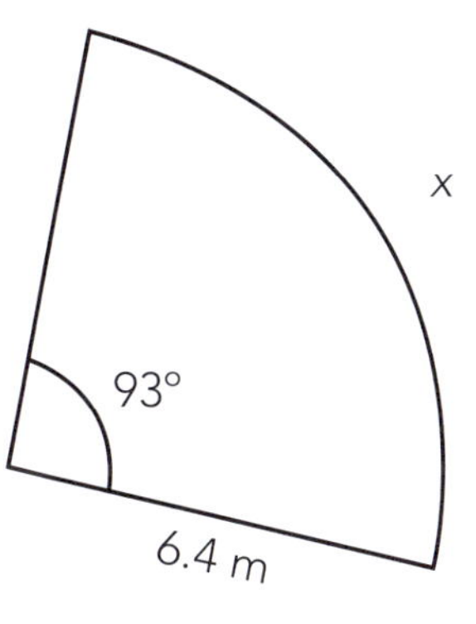

8

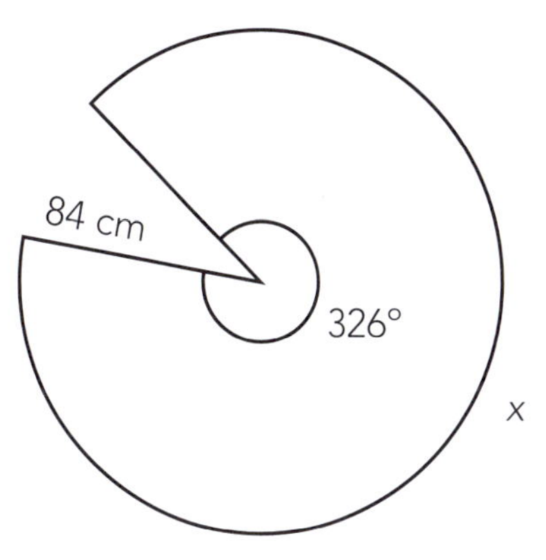

ISBN: 9780170354219

Area of a sector

You may also be required to find the area of a sector.
This is the formula to use:

$$\text{Area of a sector} = \pi r^2 \frac{\theta}{360}$$

Example: Find the area of the sector.

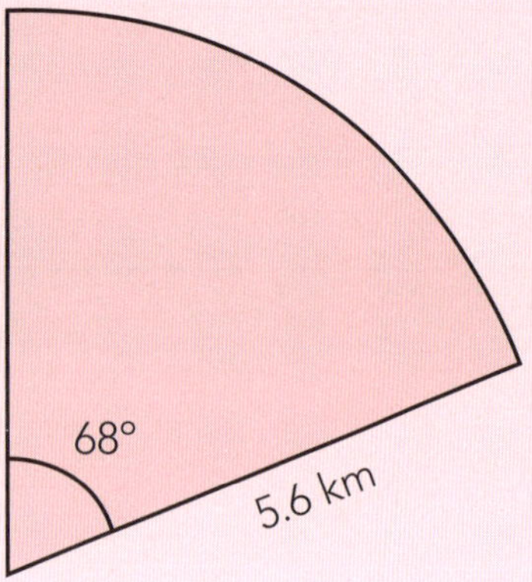

$$\text{Area of a sector} = \pi r^2 \frac{\theta}{360}$$

$$\text{Area} = \pi \times 5.6^2 \times \frac{68}{360}$$

$$\text{Area} = 18.61 \text{ km}^2 \text{ (2 dp)}$$

Find the area of these sectors.

1

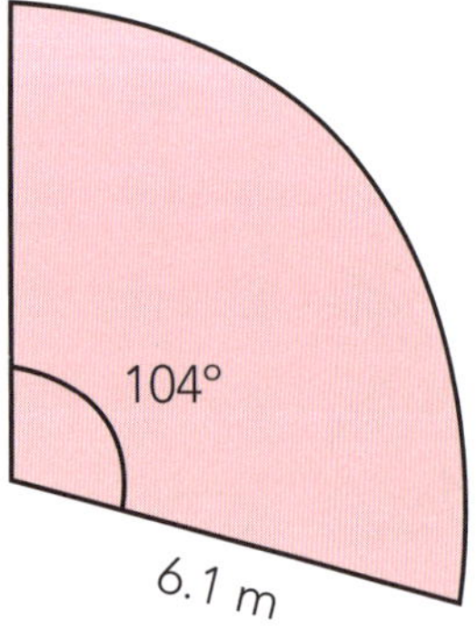

2

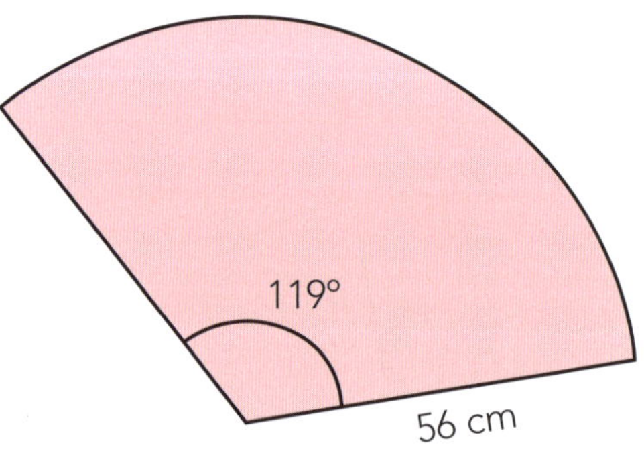

ISBN: 9780170354219

3

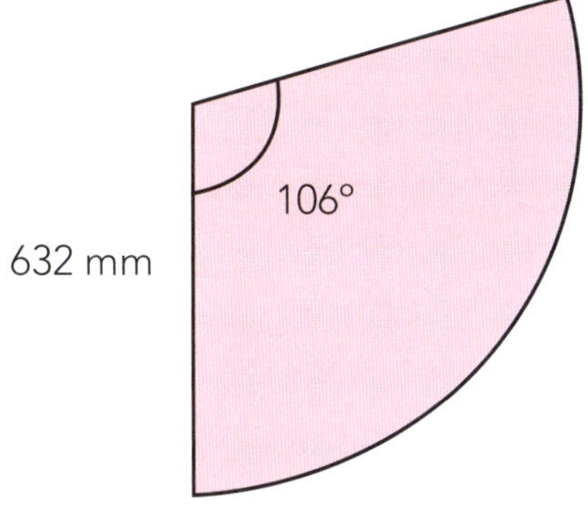

4

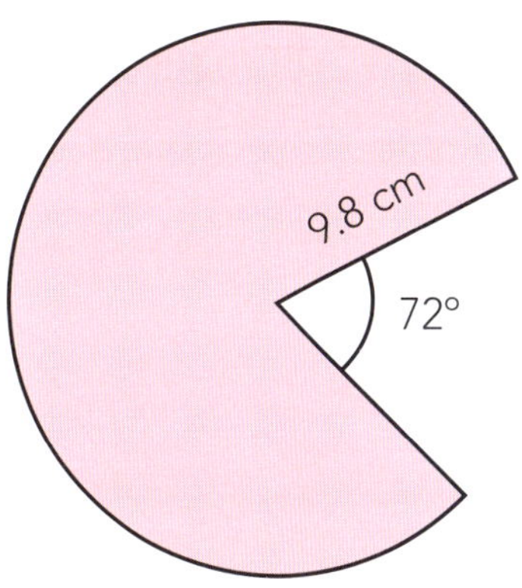

5

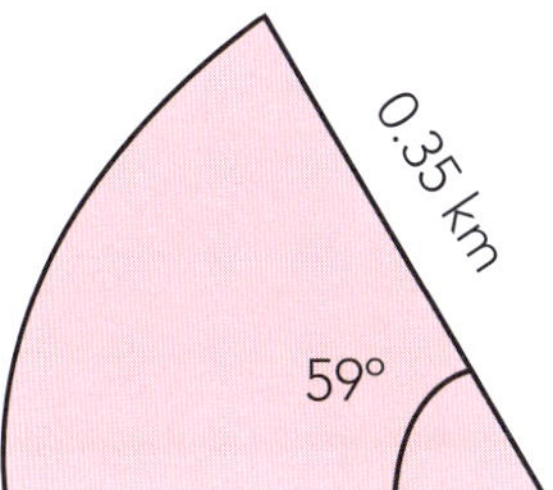

6

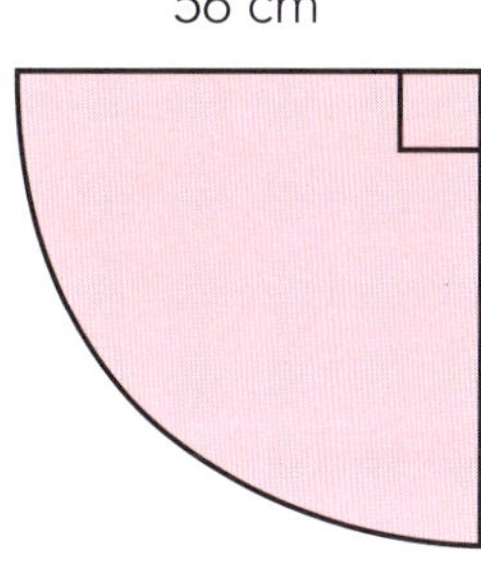

7

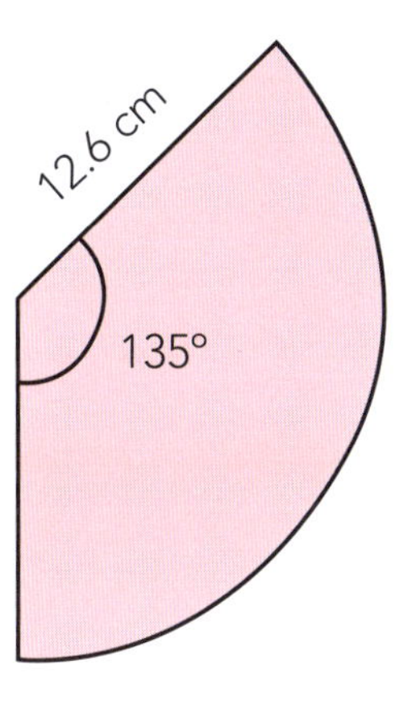

8

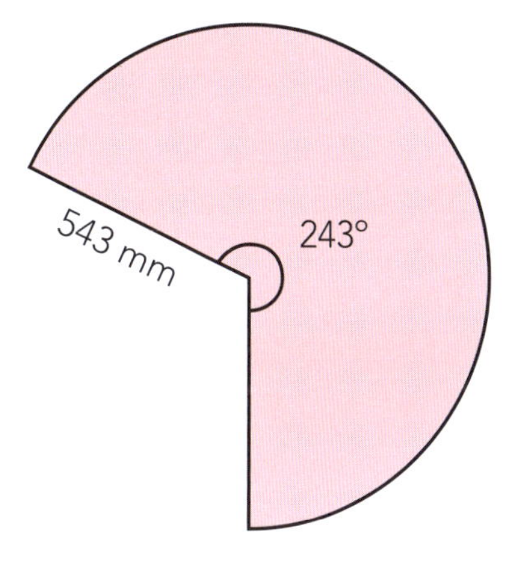

ISBN: 9780170354219

Putting it together

Find the shaded area of these shapes.

1

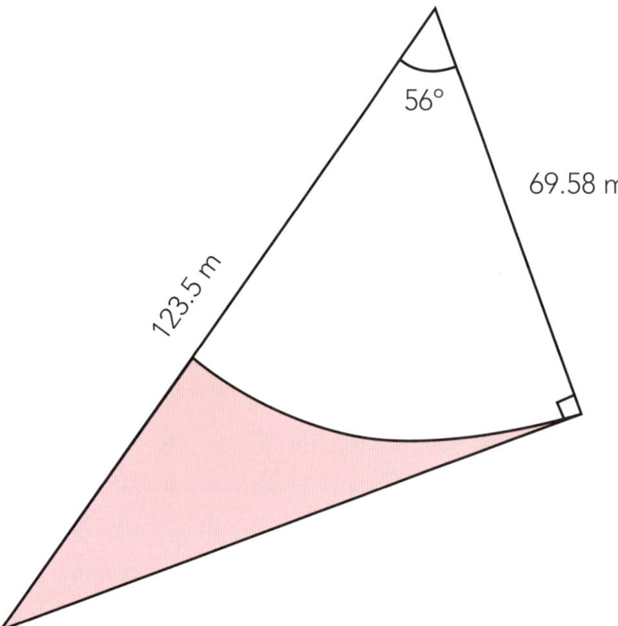

2

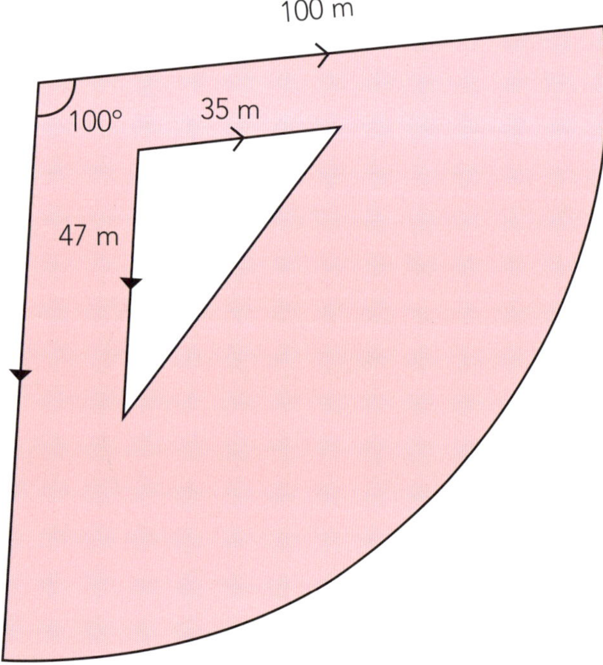

  ISBN: 9780170354219

3 A is the centre of a circle, and AB and AD are radii. BC and DC are tangents. Calculate the shaded area.

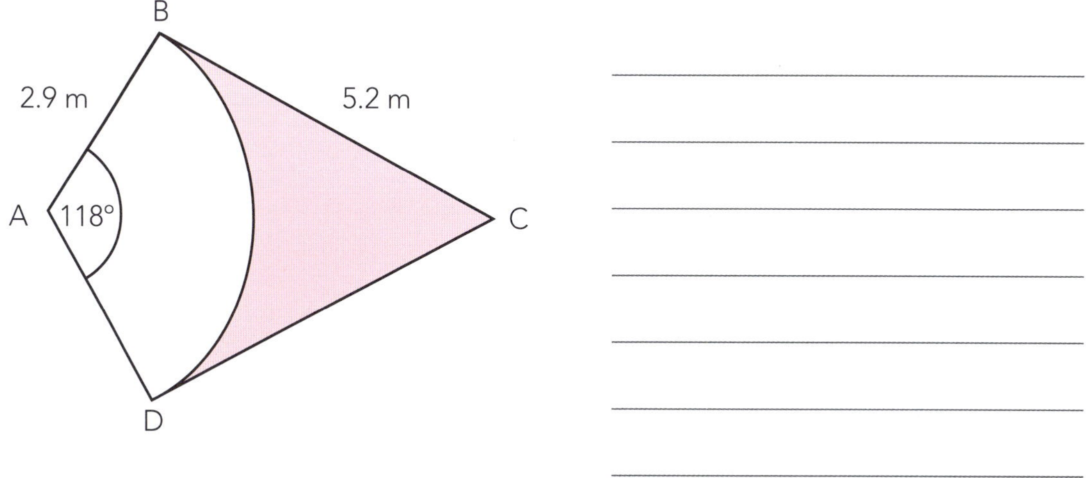

4 C is the centre of a circle which has a radius of 5 cm. CA and CB are radii and height h is 0.65 cm. The length of the arc AB is also 5 cm. Calculate the area of the shaded segment.

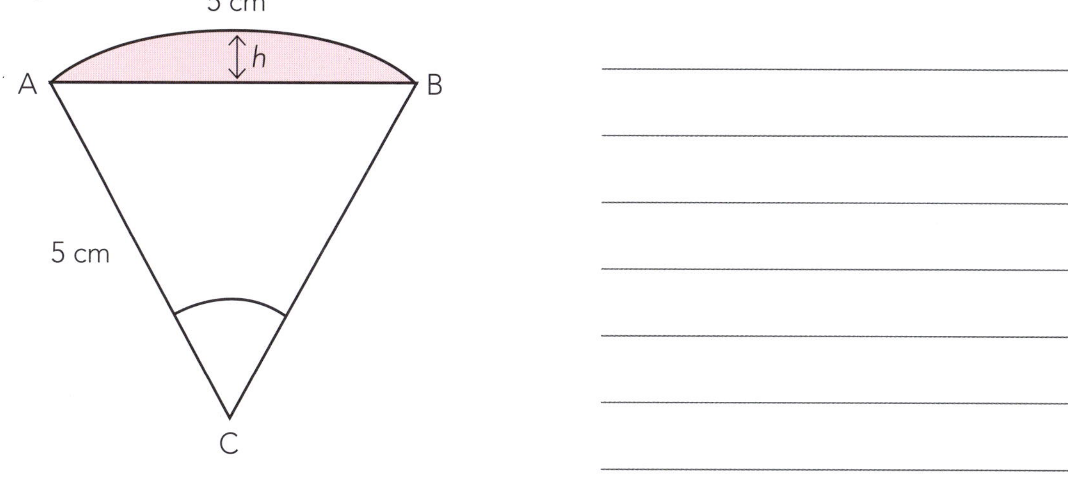

5 A sector, ABE, of a circle which has centre A and a radius of 5 cm is contained within a triangle ACD. Calculate the area and perimeter of the shaded figure.

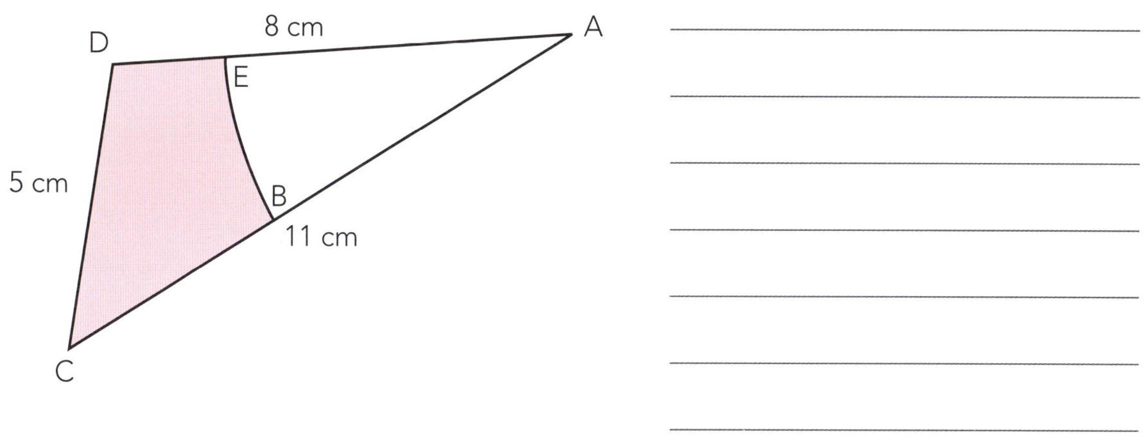

ISBN: 9780170354219

Practice tasks

Practice task one

Find the length AD.

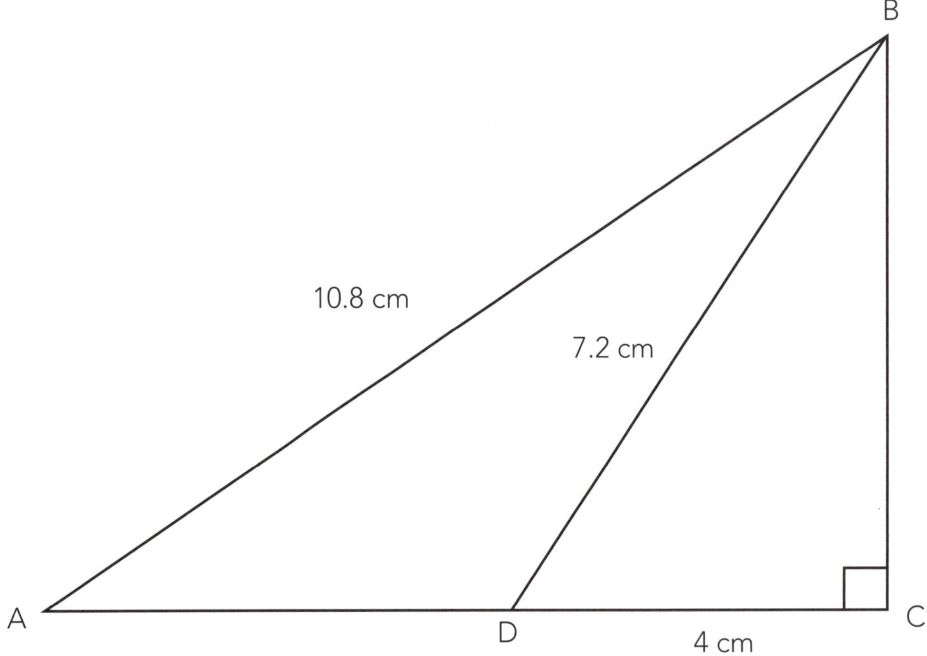

ISBN: 9780170354219

Practice task two

Find the perimeter and the area of this shape.

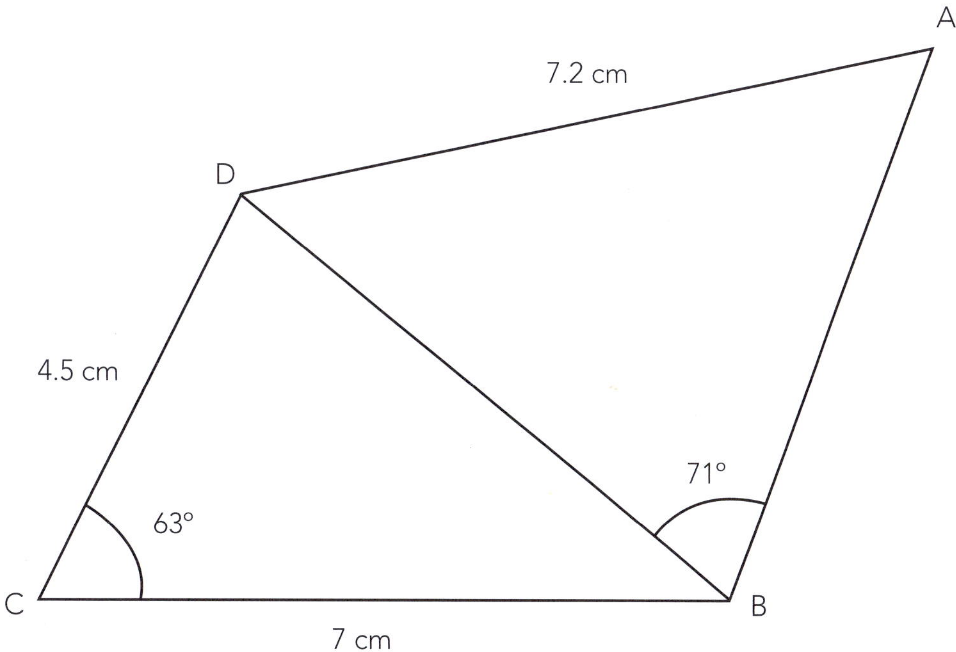

ISBN: 9780170354219

Practice task three

Calculate the difference between the areas of these triangles.

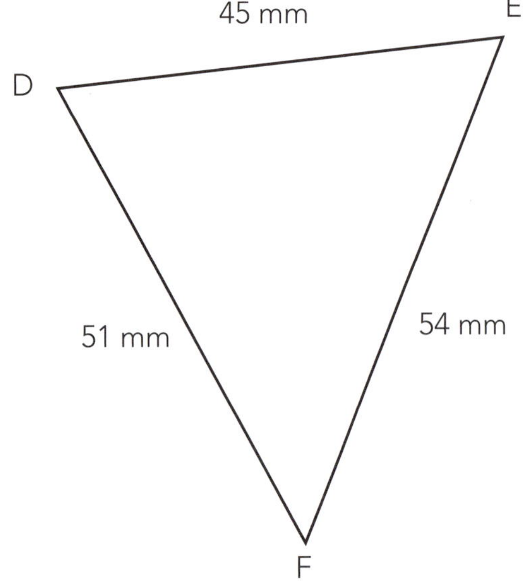

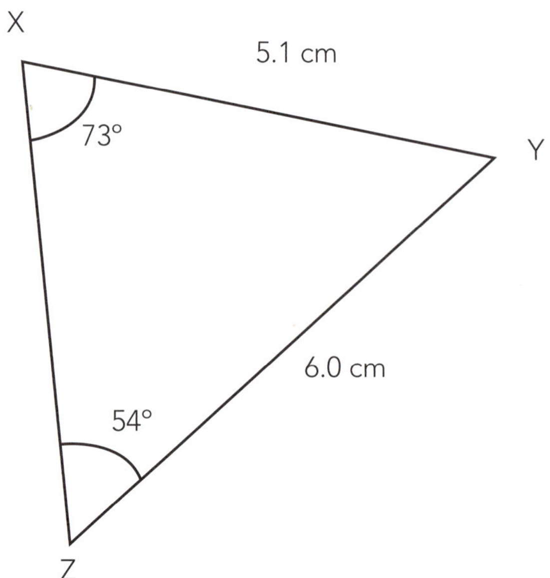

ISBN: 9780170354219

Practice task four

Find the length of AC.
Find the length of DA.
Find the area of the triangle ABC.

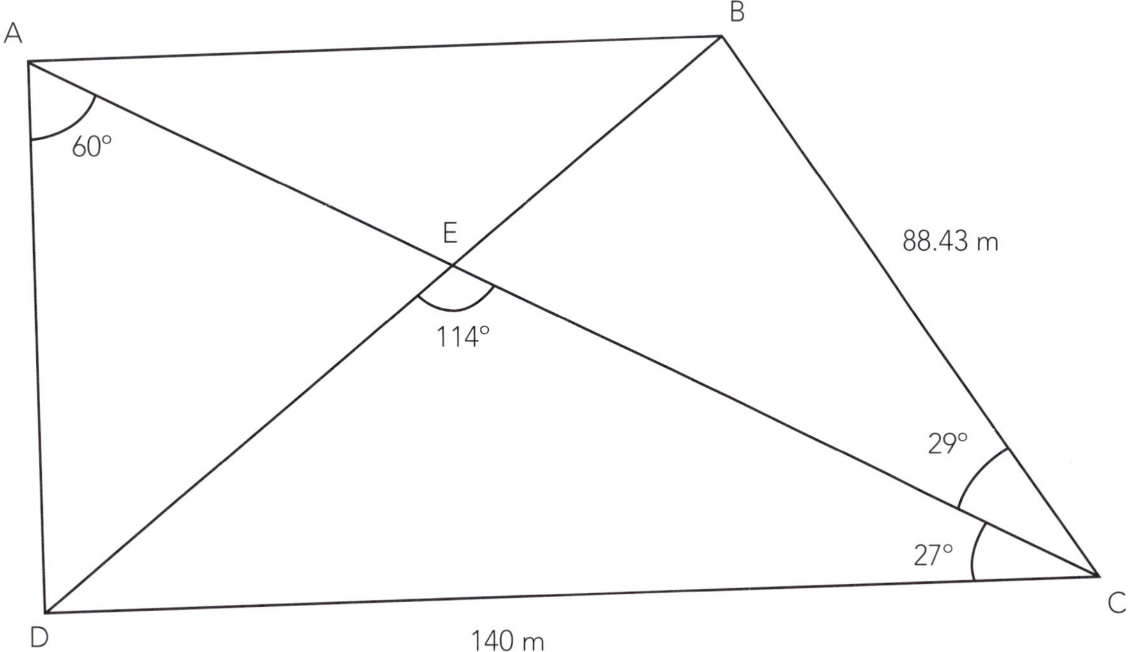

ISBN: 9780170354219

Practice task five

Find the length of YV.

Confirm that the distance around the quadrilateral WXYZ is more than 250 m.

Claudia challenges Oscar to a race from X round this course and back to X (XYZWX), however Oscar gets lost and ends up running XYVZWX.

Who has run the greatest distance?

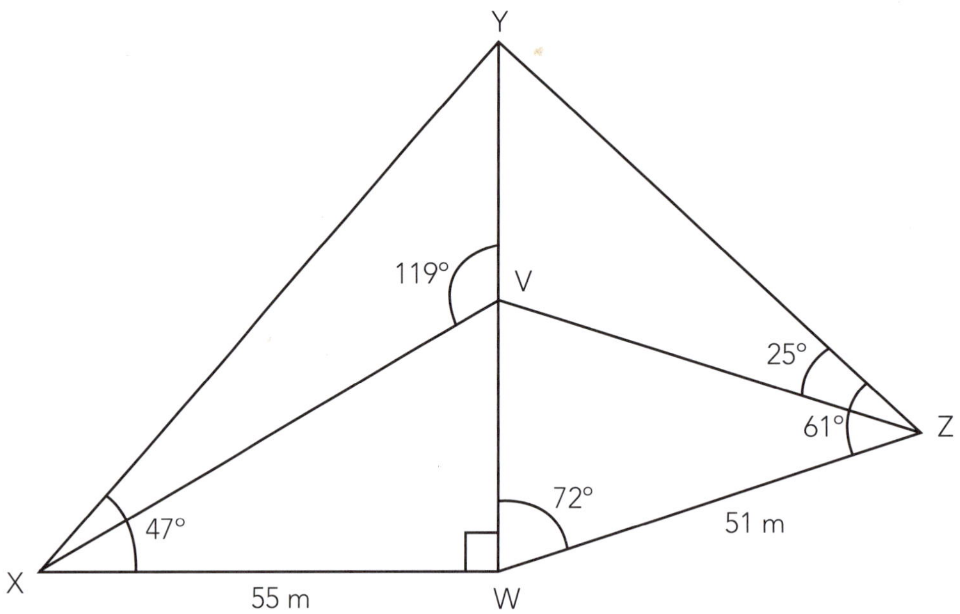

ISBN: 9780170354219

Practice task six

Angle XWZ is 48°.
Find the length of WY.
Find the area of WXYZ.

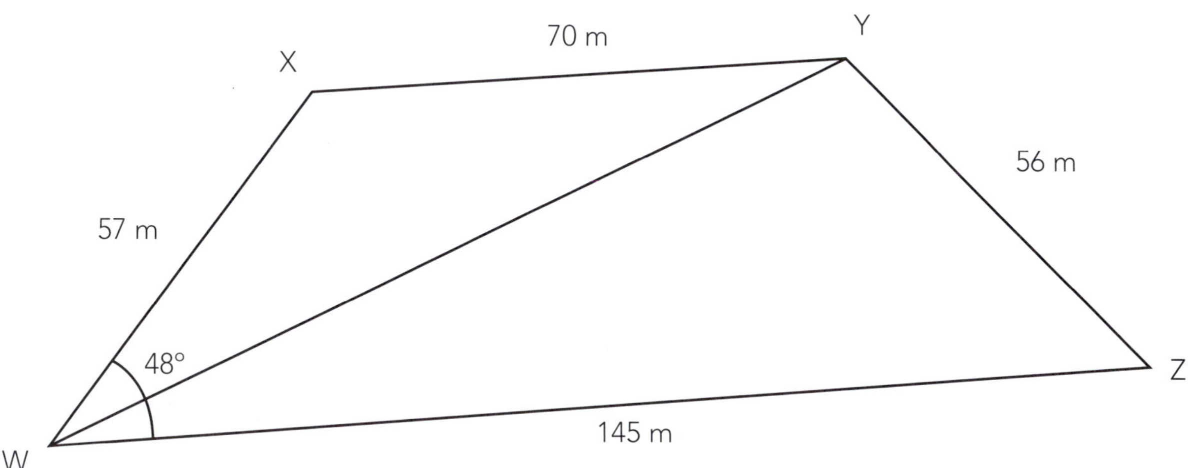

ISBN: 9780170354219

Practice task seven

On Joe's farm there is a large fenced quadrilateral-shaped paddock. Joe wants to split this paddock into three (as in the diagram).

You will need to:

- Find the external measurements of the existing paddock.
- Calculate the enclosed area.
- Find the length of fencing he will need to create these new paddocks. He has bought a 200 m roll of fencing. Is this enough for the new fence?

Joe thinks the paddocks are reasonably even (within 100 m^2). Is this the case?
If not, suggest a new split so that they are reasonably even (within 100 m^2). They do not have to remain triangular.

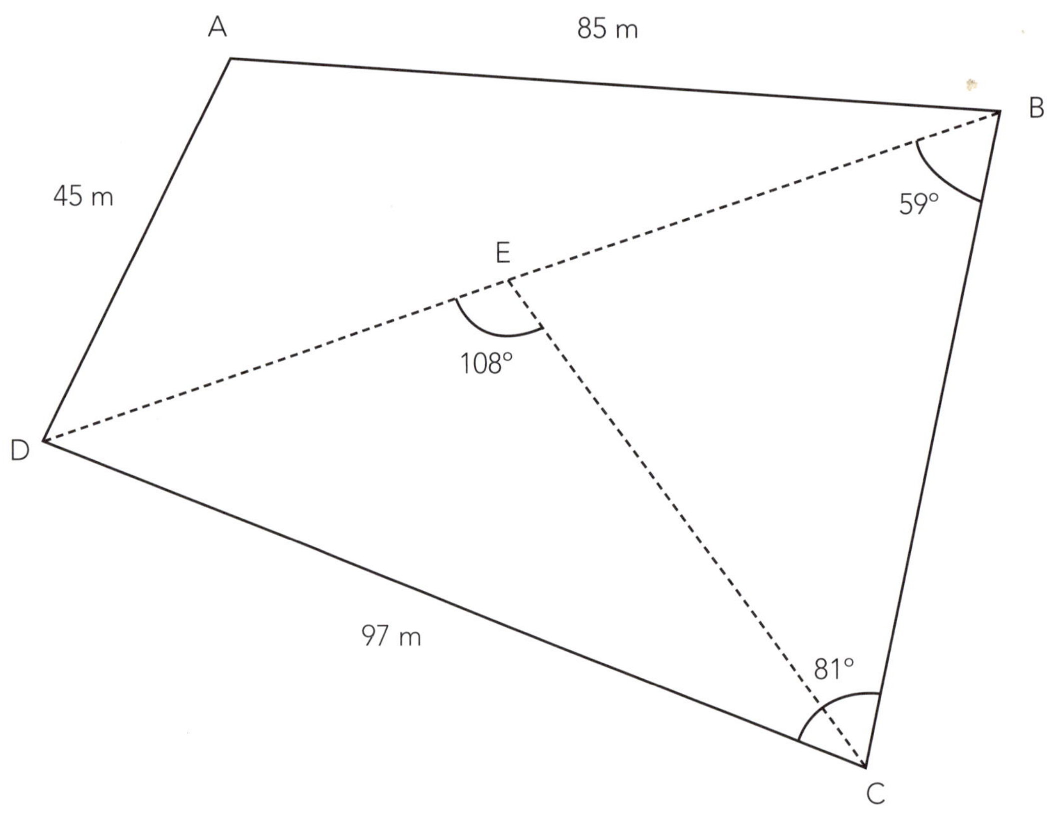

ISBN: 9780170354219

Practice task eight

This shape is symmetrical.
Find the arc length AB.
Calculate the shaded area.

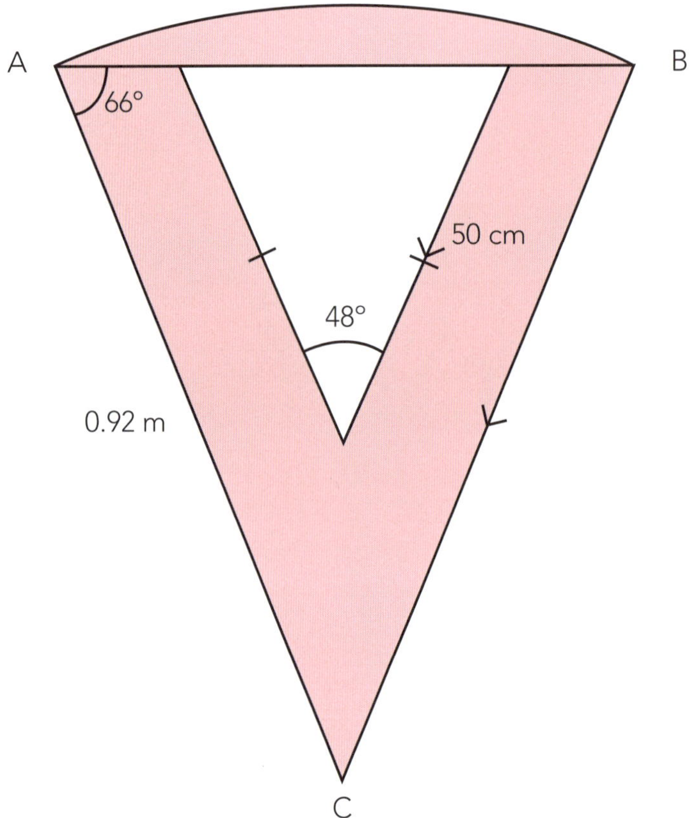

ISBN: 9780170354219

Answers

All non-integral angles are rounded to 1 dp.
All non-integral intermediate answers are rounded to 4 sf.
All non-integral final answers are rounded to 3 sf.
Professional judgement should apply.

Right-angled triangles (pp. 6–15)

Pythagoras (pp. 6–8)

1 19.2 m
2 2.65 cm
3 12.1 cm
4 7.94 cm
5 5.74 km
6 6.94 m
7 2973 m
8 20.0 m
9 393 m
10 42.4 mm
11 7.78 cm
12 10.6 cm
13 9.19 cm

Trigonometry — finding sides (pp. 9–11)

1 15.0 m
2 2.83 cm
3 2.35 cm
4 13.3 cm
5 5.98 km
6 3.36 m
7 0.726 km
8 30.7 m
9 544 m
10 46.7 mm

Trigonometry — finding angles (pp. 12–13)

1 48.6°
2 53.1°
3 26.8°
4 50.5°
5 62.3°
6 50.0°
7 45.1°
8 57.2°
9 44.2°
10 44.4°

Putting it together (pp. 14–15)

1 52.1°
2 1.72 cm
3 153 mm
4 3.14 km
5 44.2°
6 56.3°
7 8.50 km
8 12.2°
9 x = 6.36 m
y = 11.4 m
10 x = 40°
y = 70°
z = 6.84 m
11 x = 22.6°
y = 0.260 m
12 Each ridge 2.45 m Altogether = 9.80 m

Non-right-angled triangles (pp. 16–34)

Sine rule — finding sides (pp. 16–18)

1 18.3 m
2 48.4 km
3 16.0 mm
4 32.6 km
5 5.05 m
6 11.2 m
7 8.72 km
8 5.09 cm
9 24.2 mm
10 12.0 m
11 36.1 m
12 4.20 km
13 8.39 cm
14 2.22 cm
15 22.1 m
16 0.303 km

Sine rule — finding angles (pp. 19–22)

1 34.2°
2 33.7°
3 87.0°
4 52.7°
5 80.7°
6 42.7°
7 44.1°
8 63.2°
9 62.0°
10 10.1°
11 48.2°
12 78.8°

ISBN: 9780170354219

13 65.3°
14 63.5°
15 76.4°
16 61.5°
17 AC = 63.0 m
AB = 35.2 m
18 AC = 44.3 m
AD = 18.0 m

Cosine rule — finding sides (pp. 23–25)

1 2.57 cm
2 579 m
3 6.71 cm
4 34.9 m
5 6.67 km
6 119 mm
7 8.93 m
8 61.0 cm
9 5.84 m
10 229 mm
11 8.73 cm
12 10.2 km
13 3.48 cm
14 21.4 km
15 85.4 mm
16 47.2 m

Cosine rule — finding angles (pp. 26–28)

1 57.9°
2 57.1°
3 59.2°
4 61.6°
5 123.1°
6 76.2°
7 46.6°
8 70.9°
9 33.6°
10 158.2°
11 52.1°
12 41.5°
13 74.0°
14 73.0°
15 26.4°
16 81.8°

Putting it together (pp. 30–34)

1 5.59 cm
2 55.5°
3 28.7 mm
4 135.3°
5 46.2 m
6 8.11 km
7 41.2°
8 29.4°
9 32.6°
10 104.7°
11 5.91 m
12 35.6°
13 2.51 km
14 18.4 cm
15 64.8°
16 8.34 cm
17 59.2°
18 81.2 m
19 a ∠ABD = 26.5°
AB = 12.4 cm
b AC = 11.4 cm
20 AC = 4.91 cm
h = 3.92 cm
21 AC = 20.2 cm
∠DAC = 61.7°
∠CAB = 36.3°
BC = 13.3 cm
22 a AC = 106 m
AD = 39.8 m
Cliff (AE) is 41.8 m high
b DC = 98.5 m

Areas (pp. 35–41)

Triangles, other polygons and circles (pp. 35–38)

1 35 cm^2
2 60 m^2
3 1660 mm^2
4 25.2 km^2
5 952 m^2
6 36.25 m^2
7 47.9 cm^2
8 714 cm^2
9 182 km^2
10 56 cm^2
11 784 cm^2
12 4185 m^2
13 45.1 mm^2
14 75.4 km^2
15 66.0 cm^2
16 40 cm^2
17 34.9 cm^2
18 67.4 cm^2
19 53 cm^2
20 91.4 cm^2

Non-right-angled triangles (pp. 39–41)

1 10.5 cm^2
2 61.9 cm^2
3 702 mm^2
4 118 km^2
5 0.126 m^2
6 259,000 km^2
7 58.7 cm^2
8 26.9 cm^2
9 18.3 m^2
10 17.2 m^2

ISBN: 9780170354219

11 14.0 cm^2
12 316,000 mm^2
13 4.01 km^2
14 93.1 cm^2
15 1010 m^2
16 1150 cm^2
17 11.0 m^2
18 0.0109 km^2

Circular measure (pp. 42–47)

Arc length (pp. 42–43)

1. 7.99 m
2. 6.50 km
3. 167 mm
4. 170 cm
5. 10.8 km
6. 50.5 mm
7. 10.4 m
8. 478 cm

Area of a sector (pp. 44–45)

1. 33.8 m^2
2. 3260 cm^2
3. 369,000 mm^2
4. 241 cm^2
5. 0.0631 km^2
6. 2460 cm^2
7. 187 cm^2
8. 625,000 mm^2

Putting it together (p. 46–47)

1. 1180 m^2
2. 7920 m^2
3. Total area = 15.1 m^2
   Area sector = 8.66 m^2
   Shaded area = 6.42 m^2
4. Angle = 57.3°
   Area triangle = 10.5 cm^2
   Area sector = 12.5 m^2
   Shaded area = 1.98 cm^2
5. Angle A = 24.6°
   Arc length = 2.15 cm
   Perimeter = 16.1 cm
   Area triangle = 18.3 cm^2
   Area sector = 5.37 cm^2
   Shaded area = 13.0 cm^2

Practice tasks (pp. 48–56)

Practice task one (p. 48)

$\cos \angle CDB = \frac{4}{7.2}$

$\angle CDB = 56.25°$

$BC = \sqrt{7.2^2 - 4^2}$
$BC = 5.99$ cm

$x = \sqrt{10.8^2 - 5.99^2}$
$x = 4.99$ cm

Practice task two (p. 49)

$DB^2 = 7^2 + 4.5^2 - 2 \times 7 \times 4.5 \times \cos 63°$
$DB = 6.376$ cm

$\frac{\sin \angle DAB}{6.38} = \frac{\sin 71°}{7.2}$
$\angle DAB = 56.91°$

$\angle BDA = 180° - 56.91° - 71°$
$\angle BDA = 52.09°$

$\frac{AB}{\sin 52.09°} = \frac{7.2}{\sin 71°}$
$AB = 6.008$ cm

Perimeter $= 4.5 + 7 + 7.2 + 6.008$
$= 24.7$ cm

Area $\Delta CDB = \frac{1}{2} \times 7 \times 4.5 \times \sin 63°$
Area $\Delta CDB = 14.03$ cm^2

Area $\Delta DAB = \frac{1}{2} \times 6.376 \times 6.008 \times \sin 71°$
Area $\Delta DAB = 18.11$ cm^2

Total area $= 14.03 + 18.11$
$= 32.1$ cm^2

Practice task three (p. 50)

$\cos \angle FDE = \frac{51^2 + 45^2 - 54^2}{2 \times 51 \times 45}$
$\angle FDE = 68.13°$

Area $\Delta FDE = \frac{1}{2} \times 45 \times 51 \times \sin 67.27°$
Area $\Delta FDE = 1065$ mm^2

Area $\Delta XYZ = \frac{1}{2} \times 60 \times 51 \times \sin 53°$
Area $\Delta XYZ = 1222$ mm^2

Therefore ΔXYZ is 157 mm^2 larger than ΔFDE.

Practice task four (p. 51)

$\frac{AC}{\sin 93°} = \frac{140}{\sin 60°}$
$AC = 161.4$ cm
$DA = 73.39$ cm

Area $\Delta ABC = \frac{1}{2} \times 88.43 \times 161.4 \times \sin 29°$
Area $\Delta ABC = 3460$ cm^2

ISBN: 9780170354219

Practice task five (p. 52)

$\tan 47° = \frac{YW}{55}$

YW = 58.98 m

$\tan 29° = \frac{WV}{55}$

WV = 30.49 m

YW – WV = YV

YV = 28.49 m

$VZ^2 = 30.49^2 + 51^2 - 2 \times 51 \times 30.49 \times \cos 72°$

VZ = 51 m

$\cos 47° = \frac{55}{YX}$

YX = 80.65 m

$YZ^2 = 51^2 + 28.495^2 - 2 \times 51 \times 28.495 \times \cos 108°$

YZ = 65.66 m

Claudia's run = 80.65 + 65.66 + 51 + 55
= 252.3 m

Oscar's run = 80.65 + 28.49 + 50.69 + 51 + 55
= 265.8 m

Oscar runs 13.5 m further.

Practice task six (p. 53)

$ZX^2 = 57^2 + 145^2 - 2 \times 57 \times 145 \times \cos 48°$

ZX = 114.9 m

$\cos \angle YXZ = \frac{114.9^2 + 70^2 - 56^2}{2 \times 114.9 \times 70}$

∠YXZ = 21.45°

$\cos \angle WXZ = \frac{114.9^2 + 57^2 - 145^2}{2 \times 57 \times 114.9}$

∠WXZ = 110.4°

∠YXW = 131.8°

$WY^2 = 57^2 + 70^2 - 2 \times 57 \times 70 \times \cos 131.8°$

WY = 116 m

∠WZX = 21.62°

$\frac{\sin \angle XZY}{70} = \frac{\sin 21.45°}{56}$

∠XZY = 27.20°

∠ZYX = 131.3°

Area *D*XYZ $= \frac{1}{2} \times 56 \times 70 \times \sin 131.3°$

Area ΔXYZ = 1472 m^2

Area ΔWXZ $= \frac{1}{2} \times 145 \times 57 \times \sin 48°$

Area ΔWXZ = 3071 m^2

Total area of WXYZ = 4542 m^2

Practice task seven (pp. 54–55)

$\frac{DB}{\sin 81°} = \frac{97}{\sin 59°}$

DB = 111.8 m

$\frac{BC}{\sin 40°} = \frac{97}{\sin 59°}$

BC = 72.74 m

Area ΔBCD $= \frac{1}{2} \times 72.74 \times 97 \times \sin 81°$

Area *D*BCD = 3484 m^2

$\cos \angle DAB = \frac{85^2 + 45^2 - 111.8^2}{2 \times 85 \times 45}$

∠DAB = 115.1°

Area *D*DAB $= \frac{1}{2} \times 45 \times 85 \times \sin 115.1°$

Area ΔDAB = 1732 m^2

Total area of ABCD = 5216 m^2

$\frac{CE}{\sin 40°} = \frac{97}{\sin 108°}$

CE = 65.56 m

Total new fencing = CE + BD
= 177.33 m

Therefore 200 m is enough fencing.

Area ΔDEC $= \frac{1}{2} \times 65.56 \times 97 \times \sin 32°$

Area ΔDEC = 1685 m^2

Area ΔCBE = 5216 – 1684 – 1732

Area ΔCBE = 1800 m^2

No, ΔDEC is 115 m^2 smaller than ΔCBE.

Practice task eight (p. 56)

Length of arc AB $= \frac{48}{360} \times 2 \times \pi \times 0.92$

= 0.771 m

Area of sector $= \pi \times 0.92^2 \times \frac{48}{360}$

= 0.3545 m^2

Area of white Δ = 0.5 × 0.5 × 0.5 × sin 48°
= 0.0929 m^2

Area of shaded part = 0.3324 – 0.09289
= 0.262 m^2

 ISBN: 9780170354219